GLASGOW

Edited by Lucy Jenkins

First published in Great Britain in 1999 by
POETRY NOW YOUNG WRITERS
Remus House,
Coltsfoot Drive,
Woodston,
Peterborough, PE2 9JX
Telephone (01733) 890066

HB ISBN 0 75431 504 5
SB ISBN 0 75431 505 3

FOREWORD

Poetry Now Young Writers have produced poetry books in conjunction with schools for over eight years; providing a platform for talented young people to shine. This year, the Celebration 2000 collection of regional anthologies were developed with the millennium in mind.

With the nation taking stock of how far we have come, and reflecting on what we want to achieve in the future, our anthologies give a vivid insight into the thoughts and experiences of the younger generation.

We were once again impressed with the quality and attention to detail of every entry received and hope you will enjoy the poems we have decided to feature in *Celebration 2000 Glasgow* for many years to come.

CONTENTS

Jennifer Kennedy   1

Auchinloch Primary School
    Stephen Morrison   1
    Stephen Hall   2
    Euan Griffin   2
    Stacey Grant   3
    Nicola Halliday   3
    Douglas Wilson   4
    Ashleigh Burns   4
    Nicola Grant   5
    Fiona Jean Robertson   6
    Corinne Hall   6
    Sharon Devine   7

Barmulloch Primary School
    Nicole Anderson   7
    Nicolle Shaw   8
    Steven Cannon   8
    Kirsty Haigh   9
    Gary Clark   9
    Charmaine Garland   10
    Danielle Quail   10
    Gemma Gilgis   11

Chapelgreen Primary School
    Robert Morris   11
    Charlene Kirk   12
    Stuart Provan   12
    Steven McGrory   13
    Scott Rae   13
    Carly MacKenzie   14
    Garreth Boyd   14
    Robyn Reid   15
    Graeme Surgeon   15
    Christopher Scullion   16

Ben De Zutter 16
William Dunbar 17
David Barrie 17
Kirstin Brown 17

Eastbank Primary School
David Hughes 18
Craig Gordon 18
Nikki McAdam 19
Jennifer Rooney 20
Ian Hewitt 20
Lee Smith 21
Nadia McWhinnie 21
Scott Reddy 22
Gillian McCaffery 22
Laura Ballantyne 23
Leoni Conroy 23
Gemma Campbell 24
Andrew O'Neill 24
Laura Brown 25
Kirsty Mills 25
Claire Wheelhouse 26
Gillian Gray 26
Daniel McGowan 26
Sheree Christensen 27
Fiona Callaghan 27
Deborah Wood 28
Nicola Galloway 28
Danielle Dick 29
Jason King 29

Gartconner Primary School
Martin Lynch 30
Cameron Walls 30
Gillian Horn 31
Christopher Wilson 31
Jamie Carr 32
Martin Haig 32

Siobhan Richards 33
Ruth Hall 33
Louise Lamond 34
Douglas McBride 34
Blair Yates 35
Neil MacIsaac 36
Sarah Jayne Miller 36
Andrew Murphy 37
Fiona McPhail 37
Ruth Barrie 38
Andrew Morrison 38
Euan Robb 39
Andrew Pazikas 39
Jenna McBride 40
Jennifer McKenna 41
Rachel Fisher 41
Gavin Hunter 42
Kimberly Smart 42

Holy Family Primary School
Ashley McEnaney 43
Lauren McNulty 44
Kirsty Waugh 44

Househillmuir Primary School
Ross Duncan 45
Stewart Ward 45
Stephen Donnelly 46
Kelly Convery 46
Louise Greenaway 47
Natasha Picken 47

Kelvindale Primary School
Joe Lau 48
Andrew Duke 48
Pooja Varyani 49
Jane Duncan 49
Clare Sutherland 50

Shona Macmillan	50
Thomas Sutcliffe-Campo	51
Jennifer McCann	51
Laura Gray	52
Jason McMullen	52
Sean Stephen	53
Gillian Allan	53
Iain O'Donnell	54
James Sharp	54
Leah Stevenson	55
Rebecca Drummond	55
Rachel Buckley	56
Emma Makan	56
Tanya Kaur	57
Vincent Okine	57
Lyndsay Dolan	58
Garry McFarlane	58
Jaskarn Khaira	59
Nicola Hunter	59
Lewis Campbell	60
Stephanie Gray	60
Euan Maharg	61
Victoria Hay	61
Ruth Grace McKay	62
Laura Porteous	62
Michael Greenshields	63
Emily H Waddell	64
Seonaid Weightman	64
Pamela Proctor	65
Gavia Baker Whitelaw	66
Sarah Morgan	66
Emma Harkess	67
Alexandra Mellon	67
Victoria Trotter	68

Kilbowie Primary School
Katrina Raine	68
Samantha Harden	69

Stacey Paterson   69

Lairdsland Primary School
                Billy Cameron   70
                William Murray   70
                Emma Glen   71
                Sam Gilmour   71
                Lauren Horner   72
                Ben Stirling   72
                Colin MacDougall   73
                Karen Gordon   73
                Iain Boot   74
                Karen Beresford   74
                Stephanie Holbein   75
                Calvin Wilson   75

Lamlash Primary School
                Nicole Anne Welsh   76
                John McIver   76
                Steven McCarter   77
                Pamela Stewart   77

Our Lady Of The Missions Primary School
                Catherine Gillies   78
                Mary-Clare Friel   78
                Brendan McKenna   79
                Connell Duffy   80
                Eamonn Farrell   80
                Jade Corral   81
                Laura Jane Casserly   82
                Julie Hunter   83
                Mark Lyons   84
                Iain Carnegie   84
                Stephanie Boyle   85
                Lisa Dragoonis   86

Oxgang Primary School

John Hendrie	86
James Wright	87
Louise Neilson	87
Stuart McGaw	88
Christopher Connell	88

Rogerfield Primary School

Christopher Stewart	89
Sarah Allison	89
Karen McFarlane	90
Kayleigh Baldwin	90
John William Dickson	91
Kevin Paterson	91
Amanda Palmer	92
Marc Hendry	92
Jonathan Daly	93
David McClung	93
Scott Docherty	94
David Molloy	94

St Aloysius' Primary School, Springburn

Stacey McCreadie	95
Sarah Jane Queen	96
Jason Bird	97
Christopher Maguire	98
Helena Martha Walker	99
Angela Doherty	100
Gillian Skinner	101
Danielle Maguire	102

St John's Primary School

Tony Neil	102
Christy McFadden	103
Maureen McGarvey	104

St Julie's Primary School, Glasgow

Jaclyn McMahon	104
Dionne Sloan	105
Stephanie Cartwright	105
John McGinty	106
Amanda Donaghy	106
Stephanie McIntyre	107

St Leonard's Primary School, East Kilbride

Craig Mochan	107
Catriona Cameron	108
Anna Mulrain	108
Katie Park	109
Stephanie Tracey	109
Jennifer McKeown	110
Adam Jackson	110
Nicola Waddell	111
Collette Jarvie	111
Jacqueline Carroll	112
Gemma Miller	112
Linsay Waddell	113
Liam Farrell	113
David Hart	114
John Paul Rafferty	114
Katrina Duncan	115
Karen Ferguson	115
Sinead Jackson	116
Katie Thomas	116
Julianne Gallacher	117
Douglas Kerr	117
Barrie Creamer	118
Daniel Cummiskey	118
Jaimie Miller	118
Laura Brannan	119
Alexandra Carney	120

St Marnock's Primary School, Glasgow

Adam McDonald	121
Laura Smith	121
Robyn Kilcullen	122
Nichola Morris	122
Stephanie Grattan	123
Robert McCreath	123
Jamie McCann	124
Samantha Ward	124
Rachael McCreadie	125
Kayleigh McMahon	126
Claire McManus	127
Stephanie Gow	128

St Patrick's Primary School, Glasgow

Wesun Kraish	128
Sharon Bruce	129
Charles Cullen	129
Marc McCann	130
Steven Monaghan	130
Rosaleen Bans	131
Ashley McIntosh	131

St Timothy's Primary School, Glasgow

Mark McCarron	132
Mark Burke	132
Nicola Morley	132
Sarah Quinn	133
Natalie Mackin	133

Scotstoun Primary School, Glasgow

Emma Brown	134
Michael Rogers	134
Chloe Beck	134
Matthew Sharkey	135
Lauren Turner	135
Craig Worton	135
Sarah Rhodes	136

Paul McGinlay 136
Stuart Barclay 137

Shawlands Primary School
Mhairi Morrison 137
Saima Butt 138
Clair Nicholson 138
Eleanor Poyner 139
Sadia Shakoor 139
Jonathan Li 140
Neelim Gill 140
Ryan McCaig 141
Iain Hamilton 141
Neil Dinnen 142
Myles Gilpin 142
Anthony Dowridge 143
Andrew Sheddon 143
Lisa Garrity 144
Leah McKee 144
David Wilson 145
Lynsey-Anne Hutchison 145
Claire Brown 146
Linda Duncan 146
David McMahon 147
Anisa Mushtaq 147
Anna MacNaughton 148
Keith McDonald 148
Scott Jeffrey 149
Paul Leinster 149
Nadine Calder 150
Alex Finlay 150
Joanne Cairns 151
Adele Suzanne Neilson 151
Alan Bain 152
Kirin Malhi 152
Jamie McKenna 153
Alan McLaren 153
Katie O'Brien 154

Jamie Morrison	155
Jack O'Brien	155
Amy Wallace	155
Laurie Brown	156
John Peter Winchester	156
Sam Duncan	156

Stepps Primary School

Lynsey Latimer	157
Diane McKay	157
Lisa Markey	158
David Thomson	158
Jessica Louise O'Neill Murray	159
Emma Hazelton	160
Kevin McMinn	160
Megan Duff	161
Natalie C Long	162
Marisa Kerr	163
Emma-Louise Hutchison	163
Catherine O'Brien	164
Andy Paterson	164
David Hunter	165
Eilidh Gordon	166
Robert Cruickshank	166
Courtney Donaldson	167
Lorna Nicolson	168
Lauren Smith	168

Sunnyside Primary School

Donna McOnie	169
Christine Douglas	170
Tony Paterson	171
Chevonne McOnie	171
Lesley-Ann Watson	172

The Poems

LITTLE BIRD

Today I saw a little bird
all brown and chirping merrily.
Then a cat came rustling through a bush
chasing my wee friend.
I went outside to chase the cat –
'Hiss!' I said. The cat ran,
leaving the bird behind.
I went outside to help it, it was injured you see,
but I couldn't find it.
My heart sank.
I thought maybe its mum came back,
or maybe I was too late.

Jennifer Kennedy

GREEN

Green is my best colour
Because the grass is green,
And a football pitch,
And trees and peas,
And flower stems and leaves.
Green is my best colour.
I love to paint with green.
Green cars and bikes
And lorries too,
And lovely green buses.

Stephen Morrison (9)
Auchinloch Primary School

My Favourite Pet Is A Dog

Some dogs are small, some are tall,
Most dogs I know like to play with a ball.
All are different in many ways,
They do strange things some days.
Pepsi's little with a noisy bark,
He likes to run around the park.
With Zara it's plain to see,
She's much too big to sit on my knee.
But up she jumps and down she sits,
Stretches out and tries to fit.
The welcome they give makes life worthwhile,
They like to run for many a mile.
And that's why they are my favourite pets,
Except when my money gets spent at the vets!

Stephen Hall (10)
Auchinloch Primary School

Summer Days

Summer days are funny days
And the best days of our life.
The sweet flowers and bumble bees
In the summer light.
Summer sun shines all day long.
The days seem like they have never gone.
The end of the holidays have come
And back to school we go.

Euan Griffin (10)
Auchinloch Primary School

FOOTBALL

Players, players, very fit and young –
Striker and goalkeeper,
The crowd are very excited
Before the game begins.

The crowd are cheering very hard,
And now the game begins.
The centre has just been taken,
Oh! That was nearly a goal!

A penalty has been awarded –
You should have seen that foul!
Now that was an amazing goal!
The game has just finished.

Stacey Grant (9)
Auchinloch Primary School

SISTER FOR SALE

I have a sister,
But she is for sale.
She has blonde hair
And big blue eyes.
But do not be fooled –
She is the devil in disguise!
She cries day and night
And always likes to fight.
Come and have a look
At the sister for sale.

Nicola Halliday (11)
Auchinloch Primary School

SHOP TILL YOU DROP

My mum shops till she drops,
Does your mum do the same?
Every time she goes into a supermarket,
She always buys the same
And brings too much home!

My mum shops till she drops,
Does your mum do the same?
Every time she goes to town,
She always does the same –
Brings nothing home!

My mum shops till she drops,
Does your mum do the same?
Every time she goes on the computer,
She always does the same –
Orders everything online!

Douglas Wilson (11)
Auchinloch Primary School

DOGS

Birds, cats,
Fish and rats,
Are lovely pets,
But dogs are my favourite.
So cuddly and sweet,
Kind and friendly,
Big or small,
Girl or boy,
Dalmatian, Alsatian.
You need a big house,
But mine isn't.

If my house is little,
I'll have to get a small dog.
He would sleep up in my room
Beside the heater,
But he'd have to go downstairs
For food and drink.

Ashleigh Burns (9)
Auchinloch Primary School

THE BIG MATCH

We're just picking the football teams,
While the ref gets the football.
We all change into our football strips
And then run off to practise.

The day of the match quickly arrives
And supporters all line up.
Some have season tickets and some not.
All of them look for a seat.

Suddenly the ref blows the whistle.
Players go into action.
Trying our hardest to score a goal
While supporters all cheer for us.

Ref blows the whistle and it's half-time.
We get a drink of water.
Then we get ready to start again
In hope that we will win the match.

Hooray! I score a goal for the team
And supporters scream and shout.
Our team has won, the cup will be ours.
I'm the hero of the day!

Nicola Grant (11)
Auchinloch Primary School

TEACHERS!

Teachers, teachers, teachers,
what would we do without teachers?
They make you laugh,
sometimes you cry.
They work you hard,
you've got to try.
They go on courses,
to teach us more.
This must make their heads really sore.
They're always there to understand,
and will always lend a helping hand.

Fiona Jean Robertson (8)
Auchinloch Primary School

SPRING

Spring is not far away,
With more time to play.
The birds make their new nests but
My favourite thing
Is smelling the flowers.

I love to eat
My Easter Eggs
Out in the snow.
It's good to go outside
To play with all
My friends.

Corinne Hall (8)
Auchinloch Primary School

SCHOOL HOLIDAYS

The school holidays are great,
Summer is the best,
Some weeks of relaxation
And fun in the sun.

Easter is good as well,
With eggs, *yum yum!*
My Easter Hunts are great,
And back to school.

I love Christmas especially,
Because of presents. *Wow!*
The snow is whiter than polar bears,
But back to school we go!

Back to school we go – how awful,
Unhappy and grumpy.
'You have to go' our parents say.
They make us go. *Oh no!*

Sharon Devine (10)
Auchinloch Primary School

WHAT IF?

What if the streets were made of chocolate?
Would we eat all the pavements?
What if TV was made of gums?
Would we eat the TV?
What if the houses were made of hair?
Would people not see?
What if people were made of lollipops?
Would dogs and cats like to suck them?

Nicole Anderson (7)
Barmulloch Primary School

WHAT IF?

What if light was not invented?
Would you be able to see?
What if everyone was a baby?
Would there ever be silence?
What if it was only the colour white
                        that was invented?
Would the place be very colourful?
What if cars were made of balloons?
Would you float up in the air?
What if chocolate was the only thing
                        you could eat?
Would children like it?
What if grass was made of mushrooms?
Would you be able to walk on it?

Nicolle Shaw (7)
Barmulloch Primary School

WHAT IF?

What if James Bond was 21?
Would he marry Miss Crombie? Yes.
What if we were ants?
Would we be scared of birds?
What if we were robots?
Would we walk madly?
What if we were joined together?
Would we have the same blood?
What if it is James Bond's funeral?
Would Miss Crombie cry or laugh?

Steven Cannon (8)
Barmulloch Primary School

WHAT IF?

What if there wasn't an alphabet?
Would children know how to spell?
What if children were made of Smarties?
Would they be smart?
What if there was only the one times table?
Would life be easier?
What if the world was made of chocolate?
Would there be a world anymore?
What if chocolate was fruit
        and fruit was chocolate?
Would we eat fruit fruit fruit?

Kirsty Haigh (7)
Barmulloch Primary School

WHAT IF?

What if sharks were made of frost?
Would you sit on them?
What if the teachers were kangaroos?
Would they jump about all day?
What if the pubs were not invented?
Would people not get drunk?
What if girls were not invented?
Would it be quiet?

Gary Clark (7)
Barmulloch Primary School

WHAT IF?

What if tables were made of jelly?
Would children wobble about?
What if TVs were made of eggs?
Would they crack open?
What if beds were made of lights?
Would you burn yourself?
What if schools were made of numbers?
How would children be able to count?
What if streets were made of rubber?
Would you bounce about?
What if Easter eggs were made of skeletons?
Would children be scared?
What if hills were made of chocolate?
Would everyone be happy?

Charmaine Garland (7)
Barmulloch Primary School

HATS AND CATS

Nine nine nine.
The call this time
Is about a silly cat.
The firemen go up the ladders
And rescue the silly cat
And that was the end of that.

Danielle Quail (7)
Barmulloch Primary School

WHAT IF?

What if rain was made of juice?
Would children keep their mouths open?
What if walls were made of sweets?
Would children eat them?
What if schools were made of rubber?
Would everyone bounce from side to side?
What if streets were made of gold?
Would everybody dig for it?

Gemma Gilgis (7)
Barmulloch Primary School

MOVEMENTS

Slowly the sun rises in the sky
Slowly the crocodile lays its eggs
Quickly I stride back to school
Quickly the fish darts up the stream
Slowly the ants run to their anthill
Slowly the snake wiggles through the sand.

Robert Morris (9)
Chapelgreen Primary School

MY LITTLE COUSIN

My little cousin Cameron
lies quietly in his basket
surrounded by fluffy teddies.
He sits and blows tiny bubbles
and stretches his little feet.
Every time I hold his hand,
he grips tightly onto my finger.
When my papa talks
he slowly opens his clear blue eyes
and smiles.
I love my little cousin.

Charlene Kirk (10)
Chapelgreen Primary School

MY COUSIN

My cousin likes pop music
The radio blares
She tries to sing along
While we all hold our ears.
My cousin likes trendy clothes
She wears the latest fashion
Horse riding is her hobby
She likes her horse best of all.

Stuart Provan (9)
Chapelgreen Primary School

MY CLOTHES

The thing that haunts me every single night,
It lies in the corner of my bedroom,
It looks like a man waiting for me to fall asleep.
It is as if his head is in his hand.
It stands in the corner waiting to jump out on me,
Then I turn the light on.
There's only a ragged pile of clothes,
So was it a man or was it my clothes?
Nobody will ever know.

Steven McGrory (11)
Chapelgreen Primary School

SLOWLY THE . . .

Slowly the monster truck went over the rocky land,
Slowly the snail climbed up the wall,
Slowly I munch my Mars bar to keep it for longer.
The boy slowly dragged himself to school,
I dragged myself away from the TV slowly.
Slowly the tiger watched its prey.
The tortoise slowly laid its egg on the sand.
The bird slowly walked with its broken leg.

Scott Rae (10)
Chapelgreen Primary School

MY SCHOOL BAG

My school bag
Small and chubby
My companion wherever I go
It eats up my school work
It eats up my rubbish.
Now to think about it,
I should have been nicer to it.
Kicked under the table
Dragged through the dirt.
Oh, my poor little bag
Dirty with my bird's poo,
And a little worn out.
It's small, smooth and soft,
It's used as a cushion
And it's used as a seat.
Stuffed with rubbish,
I think I should have been nicer.

Carly MacKenzie (10)
Chapelgreen Primary School

BIKING

Hair streams wildly like a lion.
I race by the lovely golden fields.
Ears sting painfully as if they were ice.
Winds move quickly around you.
I love riding my fast bike.

Garreth Boyd (10)
Chapelgreen Primary School

MY SCHOOL BAG

A big black monster waiting
to eat my school books.
A dirty old dustbin,
An ugly old scavenger
waiting to eat my scraps.
But it has its good points,
Like its beautiful velvet surface,
Its soft handles to support my back.
I like my bag most of the time.

Robyn Reid (11)
Chapelgreen Primary School

SCHOOL DINNERS

The pots and pans
are hissing and spitting.
The lids jump as the food rises.
The smells and aromas
swirl round the room.
The jelly wobbles
as the dinner lady asks
'Who wants cake and lumpy custard?'

Graeme Surgeon (11)
Chapelgreen Primary School

THE DRAGON

Demon red eyes with hot flaming fire
Scaly green tail swaying side to side
Teeth as sharp as a butcher's knife
Jumping the wall spreading fire
Fire as hot as chilli
Tongue as long as a python
A roar as loud as a thunder storm
Watch out the dragon is on the prowl!

Christopher Scullion (10)
Chapelgreen Primary School

THE ICICLE

A gleaming sword has been used in a thousand battles.
It glints in the sunlight.
It hangs lonely, suspended on the edge of a cliff.
With one swift jab you could kill a knight on horseback.
But then when the sun comes out, it begins to melt away.
The ice-cold water drips off your hand.
Then the swift gleaming sword is nothing but a puddle.

Ben De Zutter (11)
Chapelgreen Primary School

SLOWLY

Slowly the tiger creeps through the woods.
Slowly the plants grow from the ground.
Slowly the ivy grows up my garden wall.
Slowly the sun rises in the sky.
Slowly the days pass to my birthday.
Slowly the snake wriggles through the long grass.

William Dunbar (9)
Chapelgreen Primary School

FIRE

Fire is a cheetah speeding through the jungle,
Spreading fiercely like a lion going for the kill.
Fire is an eagle, soaring up higher and higher
And it's a snake silently and swiftly slithering through
the jungle.
Fire is evil.

David Barrie (11)
Chapelgreen Primary School

FEAR

Fear is pitch black.
Fear tastes like salt
And it smells like sour milk.
Fear looks like a fierce puma
And it sounds like the roar of a tiger.
Fear feels like spikes on a porcupine.

Kirstin Brown (10)
Chapelgreen Primary School

COLOURS

Colours are bright
but some are dark
and not as bright as a light.
Or a dark piece of bark
mix it with white
or mix it with black
and white will turn it really light
or mix it with black and it will turn to dark.
Green is my favourite
blue's second best,
green on a hair net
or blue on a test.
Colour in pictures, red, blue and green,
this is the end
of the colours you've seen.

David Hughes (9)
Eastbank Primary School

FOOTBALL

F ootball is such fun to play
O n Saturday and Sunday
O r during school. At
T raining we always do exercises and
B ench sit-ups
A nd play
L ongres. At the weekend I have a
L ong journey to Ibrox to watch Rangers
    beat every team.

Craig Gordon (10)
Eastbank Primary School

ME!

I never thought I would be here this day,
To see my friends, to go out to play,
To move my arms, legs and even talk,
To run a mile and then just walk.
Do all the sports I do,
Dance and dance till I turn blue.
I can even eat, drink and sleep,
Hop, jump and leap.
Sing – *mmm*, just wait a minute,
I'm very good with my rubbish – I always bin it.
I am kind to others,
I have a couple of brothers.
I like my music band,
I think they're the best in the land.
My name's Nikki,
But my mum calls me 'Tricky Nikki'.
Why do I have to be me?
I've always wondered where I would be
without my loved ones.
My favourite fruit would have to be plums,
Mostly the ones which are green,
And I try not to be mean!
I'm quite good, don't be mistaken,
My best crisps are smoky bacon.

I will have to say
'No one can change me
and I am who I am.'

Nikki McAdam (10)
Eastbank Primary School

HENRY, MY GUINEA PIG

Henry, Henry, my black, brown and white guinea pig.
He eats his food which is so, so good.
He lies in his bed and runs about mad.
Oh Henry, Henry, you are so, so mad.
At night he sleeps alone in the dark,
Which is better than sleeping in a big park.
Oh Henry, Henry, I love you so,
I love Henry and he loves me.
He cuddles me and nibbles my finger,
That's why I love him so.

Jennifer Rooney (10)
Eastbank Primary School

UNTITLED

One day when I was going to the shop
I fell down a massive drop.
I don't know how, I don't know why
I had a bruised leg and a black eye.

Flying birdies around my head
For a minute I thought I was dead.
I don't know why, I don't know how
When I got up, I turned into a cow.

Ian Hewitt (10)
Eastbank Primary School

FOUR LITTLE TIGERS

Four little tigers
Sitting in a tree
One became a lady's coat
And now there's only three.

Three little tigers
Beneath a sky of blue
One became a rich man's rug
Now there's only two.

Two little tigers
Sitting in the sun
One a hunter's trophy made
Now there's only one.

One little tiger
Waiting to be had
Oops! He got the hunter first
Aren't you kind of glad?

Lee Smith (10)
Eastbank Primary School

SPRING IS HERE

It's nearly spring,
The flowers are nearly out.
There's a lot of green and colour about.
Daffodils, crocus and snowdrops
Make it a much brighter world
To live in.

Nadia McWhinnie (10)
Eastbank Primary School

BASKETBALL

Basketball is my favourite sport
I don't know why
you throw the ball
you bounce the ball
I wonder why?

I play it every day and night
I throw the ball to the net
it bounces up and down
until it goes right in the net.

By the time I am finished
I have a big score
I am very proud of myself
and everyone else is too.

The big day came
I was in a team
I scored lots of goals
we all won the game.

Scott Reddy (10)
Eastbank Primary School

THE FUNNY WONDERLAND

In a place called Wonderland
It is a funny looking place
Full of funny things that look out of place.
In this funny place where everything looks out of place
People with funny little faces
Live in funny little places.

Gillian McCaffery (10)
Eastbank Primary School

MILLENNIUM BUG

M assive traffic jams due to traffic light failure
I ll people at risk as monitors fail
L ights going out all over the world
L iving in fear of the year 2000
E nd of a century, start of a new
N umerous disasters are waiting to happen
N o more fun as the TV goes blank
I s it going to be as bad as we are made to believe?
U p in the sky the satellites die
M artians could land and no one would know

B usinesses in chaos as Wall Street crashes
U tter confusion all over the world
G o and rejoice, this was only a dream!

Laura Ballantyne (10)
Eastbank Primary School

CHOCOLATE

C hocolate, chocolate
H ot or cold
O f
C ourse when I eat it I go
O ver the moon
L ovely chocolate
A lways
T astes delicious
E very time.

Leoni Conroy (10)
Eastbank Primary School

SPACE

Way up there
Above us all
Very big and
Very tall

They're all up there
We cannot see
What they're doing
To you or me

They all shine bright
They all are small
They're not very wide
And not very tall

They are
The sun, the sky, the moon, the stars,
Jupiter, Neptune and Mars
Earth is our planet
We should be glad to have it.

Gemma Campbell (10)
Eastbank Primary School

SPACE

Our S olar system has different things
        P lanets big and small
        A steroids that are big and wide
Mer C ury the hottest and closest planet to the Sun
And E arth our living home.

Andrew O'Neill (10)
Eastbank Primary School

MY DOLPHIN POEM

D olphins are my favourite sea animal. They swim
O n top of and underneath the sea. Dolphins are
L ovely animals. They are very
P layful animals. They live in
H uge groups. Dolphins are very
I ntelligent and clever animals. Bottle-
N osed dolphins are my favourite kind of dolphins
S wimming in the sea.

Laura Brown (10)
Eastbank Primary School

THE BIG RED BALLOON

A man and his wife went to the moon
Up they went in a big red balloon.
Up, up and away high they did fly
Right up through the clouds so high,
The light was so bright with the stars in the sky.
They had laughs and fun all the way,
They reached the moon, let down the balloon
                        and decided to stay.

Kirsty Mills (10)
Eastbank Primary School

CLAIRE

C lever and kind
L ikes to swim
A nimal lover
I rish dancer
R ubbish at football
E njoys PE.

Claire Wheelhouse (10)
Eastbank Primary School

PLUTO

P luto is the smallest planet
L ittle Pluto in the sky
U nder the sun or over the moon
T oo small, so it is
O n the pictures we learn more about
        Pluto.

Gillian Gray (10)
Eastbank Primary School

DANIEL

D elightfully happy
A nimal lover
N ice little chappie
I ntelligent little brother
E ndlessly chatty
L oves his mother.

Daniel McGowan (9)
Eastbank Primary School

WHEN I GROW UP

When I grow up
I think I'll be
A detective

I could be a soldier
Or a sailor too
I'd like to be a keeper
At the public zoo

I'll own a trumpet
And I'll play a tune
I'll keep a spaceship
To explore the moon

I would like to be
A teacher but not a
Creature.

Sheree Christensen (10)
Eastbank Primary School

THE ALIEN

I went to the sweet shop to get some sweets
When I saw an alien walking down my street
It took me to its spaceship
And said, 'My name is Kip.'
I put on my spacesuit
And then my boots
5 4 3 2 1 blast off!
We're off.

Fiona Callaghan (10)
Eastbank Primary School

MY FRIEND THE ALIEN

My friend the alien comes from Mars,
My friend the alien has three different cars,
My friend the alien likes my dog,
My friend the alien can turn into a log,
My friend the alien eats all day,
My friend the alien wants to stay,
My friend the alien likes my school,
My friend the alien plays me at pool,
My friend the alien went to France,
My friend the alien learnt to dance,
My friend the alien likes to run,
My friend the alien ate a bun,
My friend the alien has a comb,
My friend the alien has to go home,
My friend the alien said bye bye,
My friend the alien is up in the sky.

Deborah Wood (10)
Eastbank Primary School

SCHOOL

School, school it is cool,
Not to talk or break the rules,
To work hard and get the grades,
Now a teacher's pet's been made,
To work clear and precise,
Our teacher's really nice,
Our topic is now on space,
Now all our teachers have lost the place.

Nicola Galloway (10)
Eastbank Primary School

SCHOOL DINNERS

S chool dinners
C hewy carrots
H orribly runny peas
O h, what about stewed steak!
O range juice, yum yum
L ovely fish and chips.

D readed lasagne
I cky sticky fudge cake
kN ickerbocker glory
N ippy chicken curry
E ggs in a cup
R otten runny beans
S crumptious crispy cake.

Danielle Dick (10)
Eastbank Primary School

JASON

J ogging all the time
A nimal lover too
S uper at work
O n the go all the time
N ever angry when it snows.

Jason King (10)
Eastbank Primary School

FOOTBALL

Footy is a great sport
The pass of the ball
The wind in your hair
And all of the goals

That madness you get
With the ball at your feet
The mud on your shirt
Your water-logged boots

Foul in the box
It's a penalty shot
It's me up next
I draw to the ball
I shoot I . . .
oooh no!

Martin Lynch (11)
Gartconner Primary School

REALLY BORED?

        Really bored,
        Really bored,
Put some custard under your shoe,
Fill your pockets full of ink,
Drive a nail through your cat's tail,
Wash your hair with lots of soup,
Juggle your toys down your stairs,
Stick some cheese inside your watch,
Eat some rats beside a hungry bear,
Put some marbles under the doormat.

Cameron Walls (10)
Gartconner Primary School

WE'VE GOT SUCH A DORKY TEACHER

Our teacher is such a geek,
She has thick black-rimmed glasses,
And loads of jotters piled in masses,
Sometimes her big buck-teeth show,
And when you ask her a question, her face will glow.

When she rubs the blackboard, the chalk goes in her face,
And when she smiles at you, you can see her brace.
When it comes to doing Topic,
Her education is catastrophic.

She has a spot at the end of her nose,
And *wow!* How wide are those toes?
We all wish she'd just go away,
Luckily she's going to Africa next May.
                              (We can't wait!)

Gillian Horn (11)
Gartconner Primary School

HOMER SIMPSON

Homer Simpson is very jolly,
He loves to skate about on a trolley.
He likes to watch TV, just like you and me,
Homer likes to eat pork chops in big juicy slops.
He likes to scoff a whole load of doughnut,
Especially with jam and nuts.
He loves his daughter Lisa the best, because she's always right,
He hates Bart because he thinks he's not smart.
He really loves his wife Marge because she makes pork chops.

Christopher Wilson (10)
Gartconner Primary School

THE UNUSUAL THING

The unusual thing,
The unusual thing,
It acts as if it is a king.
Its blood is kind of bluish-black,
Its eyes are red and yellow,
Its tentacles are green and blue,
Its scales are pink and purple.
It has 23 fingers
And 42 toes.
Whatever is this creature?
Nobody knows.

Jamie Carr (10)
Gartconner Primary School

FRUIT

Fruit has many colours,
Green, yellow, orange, red and purple.
There are also lots of names,
Pineapples, apples, bananas and strawberries.
Yummmmmmm.

Fruit is good for you
And tastes brilliant.
I wish I had one just now.

PS - I love fruit.

Martin Haig (10)
Gartconner Primary School

HAPPINESS

Happiness is when I have a long lay-in.
Happiness is when I see my dad.
Happiness is when Rangers lose.
Happiness is when I play with my friends.
Happiness is when I see my cousins.
Happiness is when it is my birthday.
Happiness is when it is Easter.
Happiness is when it is Christmas.
Happiness is when it is the summer holidays.
Happiness is when people stay overnight with me.

Siobhan Richards (10)
Gartconner Primary School

HAPPINESS

Happiness is Christmas Day,
Having my family come to stay,
Hearing the birds sing outside,
Lovely thoughts on my mind,
A piece of delicious cake that never ends,
Playing games with my friends,
Going on holiday in the sun,
Singing and dancing and having fun.

Ruth Hall (10)
Gartconner Primary School

My Worst And Best Day At School Ever

This morning I woke up, I was feeling sick,
No time for breakfast – bus is here – quick.
On the bus not feeling happy,
Everybody else is feeling chatty.

First lesson German, everything is going right,
Until I got into a fight with my partner
Over a pencil sharpener.

Next lesson Topic, which is on electricity,
Outside the wind is blowing busily.
Then we hear a scream from the teacher,
We thought it was a dream as she went up in flames.
'Hey!' someone shouted, 'let's all play games.'

The day hasn't turned out bad after all,
I'm now going home to play football,
With a kick and a shout,
Everyone running about.

Then we decide to play dodgy ball,
Running and jumping, just missing the ball.
You see, we had fun shouting,
Jumping, running and all.

Louise Lamond (11)
Gartconner Primary School

Year 2000

The year 2000 is coming soon,
This only happens once in a blue moon.
It makes me want to jump with glee,
If you look I'll jump, you'll see.

New Year is going to be so cool,
If you miss it, you'll be a fool.
I'll only see the millennium once,
If I missed it I'd be a dunce!

Douglas McBride (10)
Gartconner Primary School

MY HAMSTER (GIOVANNI)

My hamster is cute and furry, has sharp teeth
and a black and white coat.
He runs up his ladder to his food bowl,
He dives for it and starts munching and crunching.
Giovanni then jumps off the second floor of his cage,
Does a roly-poly in the air and lands on his back.
He lets out a squeal, gets up and starts running about even more.
Giovanni climbs up the side of his cage,
Climbs up so he is hanging from the roof like 'hang tough'on
                                    'Gladiators'.
I open his cage door to put him in his ball.
He drops down and runs for the door.
Before he can get away, I make a grab for him.
I open the door of the ball and plop him inside.
As soon as I put him in, he clambers back out,
'No, I've lost Giovanni!'
I search for him everywhere.
One last place!
I run into my bedroom and find him curled up in a ball
sleeping on my bed.

Blair Yates (11)
Gartconner Primary School

HAPPINESS IS . . .

Happiness is a good day out.
Happiness is no maths or language for a day.
Happiness is doing art.
Happiness is Saturday and Sunday.
Happiness is a new day of fun.
Happiness is football after school.
Happiness is playtime.
Happiness is a new topic.
Happiness is to play a fun game
                    with Scott, my friend.

Neil MacIsaac (10)
Gartconner Primary School

HAPPINESS

Happiness is seeing Henrik Larsson score,
Happiness is swimming 80 lengths,
Happiness is eating salt & vinegar crisps,
Happiness is when I go on holiday,
Happiness is playing with my best friend,
Happiness is seeing my brother happy,
Happiness is when my cousins came to stay,
Happiness will be getting my dog!

Sarah Jayne Miller (10)
Gartconner Primary School

MENORCA!

We're going to Menorca!
Off the sunny Spanish shore.
But we'd better get a move on,
Quick! Get out the door.

Look! We're flying over France, Belgium
And the English Channel too,
I've just stepped off the flamin' plane
And I really need the loo.

Our hotel is really up-market,
There's an outdoor swimming pool,
I'm off to play football on the beach,
Cos I really can't keep cool!

Before you know it, you're home again
And you're in boring old school,
But you wish that you were back in Spain
Relaxing in the pool!

Andrew Murphy (11)
Gartconner Primary School

MY CAT

My cat has black silky fur,
When he is happy he likes to purr!
He gives me a cuddle, then we snuggle down,
He often gets a fright in the middle of the night.
I love him so much.

Fiona McPhail (10)
Gartconner Primary School

FRIENDSHIP

Fiona is her name,
Our friendship isn't a game.
Fiona is so cool,
I met her first at school.
We like to go out to play,
Every single day.
My friend used to be Laura Burt,
She'd help me too if I was hurt.
Ruth is kind as well,
She is nice, you can tell.
These are just some of my friends,
And they are *very special* to me.

Ruth Barrie (10)
Gartconner Primary School

CARS

A Jaguar is a very fine car,
I should know, I have been in one.
My dad's best friend has a Mercedes Benz.
An F16 is like the queen of all cars.
A Rolls Royce is probably the choice of car
                    for the Prime Minister.
A limousine is transport for Queen Elizabeth the second.
A Cosworth is a very fine car, I must say!
A Peugeot 306 is a massive car I've heard.
Though I think all cars are good.

Andrew Morrison (10)
Gartconner Primary School

MONDAY RUSH

'*Ahh!* Look at the time, it's 8 o'clock
and I am still in bed.'
'Oh no!' says Mum as the toaster blows up.
'Euan, hurry up and have some breakfast,' says Dad
as I run half-dressed down the stairs.
'*Ahh!* The hamster's escaped!' shouts Fraser.
'It's fallen asleep in my slipper!' shouts Mum.
'Stop shouting!' shouts Dad.
Bang! goes the kettle as it falls on the floor.
All the hot water pours out and burns Dad's foot.
It's a minute to 9, I get a lift to school
and I make it just in time.

Euan Robb (11)
Gartconner Primary School

HERCULES PLOD

Hercules Plod is rather odd,
His eyes are red, his nose is blue,
His neck and head are joined by glue.
He only eats on upturned peas,
Bacon rings and melted cheese.
He rarely talks and never smiles
But goes for walks with crocodiles.

Andrew Pazikas (10)
Gartconner Primary School

SPIDERS!

Spider on the wall!
Spider in the bath!
Spider tickling your feet at night,
Makes you want to laugh.

Like tiny little monsters,
Eight little legs with feet,
If you have arachnaphobia,
You'll scream if a spider you should meet.

There are hundreds of thousands of spiders,
Some of you don't want to know,
But no matter how hard you try,
Out of the house they'll *never* go!

You can flush them down the toilet,
You can spray them with the hose,
But more and more will keep coming,
From where, *nobody* knows!

They're under rocks, they're in the trees,
They're in your garden shed!
They're in your house, they're on the wall,
They're on the ceiling above your bed!

So whatever you do . . .
Don't upset a spider!

Jenna McBride (11)
Gartconner Primary School

MY MUM

My mum's pure mad,
And I'm quite glad,
She's also incredibly nutty,
She has loads of friends,
Drives fast round the bends.
Last week she made a chip butty.

Mum is really into pop,
And only buys CDs if they're at the top.
She is sometimes really funny,
And likes it when it's really sunny.

I suppose you could say she is a bit like me,
Sometimes funny and enjoys a good party.
She is all these things, so don't say she's not,
Because she is my mum and I love her a lot.

Jennifer McKenna (11)
Gartconner Primary School

WATER

Dripping down *plop plop plop,*
Out of the tap and into my bath,
Getting full now,
Really warm,
Time to get into my
Hot cosy bath,
On a cold winter's night.

Rachel Fisher (11)
Gartconner Primary School

SPACE

Space, space
Is such a wonderful place,
With Earth and Mars
And the brightness of stars.

In space there are ten different planets
Of which Mercury is a gannet (for heat of course).
Mercury is the closest planet to the sun,
What if they clashed together, now that would be fun!

Astronauts normally go to the moon,
Well they try.
If I had to go on a rocket to the moon,
I would hope to get there very soon.

Gavin Hunter (11)
Gartconner Primary School

MY LITTLE TABBY CAT

I have a little tabby cat,
She is just seven years old.
She likes to sleep beside the fire
To keep away the cold.
She runs around the house at night,
She likes to jump and play,
But in the morning when I wake,
She likes to sleep all day.

Kimberly Smart (11)
Gartconner Primary School

THE MILLENNIUM IS COMING

The millennium is coming
Parties everywhere
The millennium is coming
Fireworks in the air.

Jumping on the chairs
Dancing all around
What a happy time it will be
When I hear the bells sound.

I will be joyful when the millennium comes
And that I am there
But even if you are not somewhere special
Do not despair.

For it will still be a wonderful time
No need to shed a tear
Because when you hear the great dong of Big Ben
A new era will be here.

I will be with my family
At a party somewhere
And when the millennium comes
It will be a time to share.

I hope the millennium will be peaceful
No wars or anything wrong
I hope it will be the best century ever
We have waited for this chance for so long.

It will be the beginning of a new century
A new start for everyone
A chance to put things right
A new life under the sun.

Ashley McEnaney (10)
Holy Family Primary School

THE YEAR 2000

The fireworks shoot up and then go pop
Will this excitement ever stop?
The party attracts people from a very wide range,
But will the world really change?
Big Ben chimes, hats fly up in the air,
People running and shouting without a care.

Not even animals are curled under a stone,
They're up throwing a huge celebration, a party of their own.
Everybody is having so much fun,
I can't wait till the year 2001.
It's so late and everybody's tired,
Oh good, the last firework's been fired.

Everybody's heading back to their car
But when they find out it's not working, they will not get far.
When they get home, just as they fear,
All over the world the Millennium Bug is here.
No power at all seems to be on,
I'll stay for a while but the question is how long?

Lauren McNulty (10)
Holy Family Primary School

THE MILLENNIUM

The millennium is coming
The millennium is coming
Parties, dancing all night long
Maybe someone will get up and
give us a song.

Everyone will have such fun,
Dancing to the rise of the sun,
I'll be in England, that's where I'll be,
That's what the millennium means to me!

Kirsty Waugh (11)
Holy Family Primary School

CRUISING KOSOVO

The peace deal failed
Cruise missiles
Air strikes
No hope of peace
Refugees on the move
Rebels in the hills
Villages on fire.

Ross Duncan (10)
Househillmuir Primary School

WAR BUT NOT PEACE

America and Britain
Went to war
Against the Serbians
Because they wouldn't sign
A peace agreement
And wouldn't stop bombing Kosovo.

Stewart Ward (10)
Househillmuir Primary School

FIGHT FOR LIVES

Last night,
Britain and America
Went to war
Against the Serbians.
Last night
They wouldn't sign
For peace.
They wouldn't
Stop killing
In Kosovo.
The war started
Last night.

Stephen Donnelly (10)
Househillmuir Primary School

CENSUS

Sixty million people
Living on our island
Fill in a form
Every 10 years
Everything written
Is a secret
Stored on a shelf
27 miles long.

Kelly Convery (10)
Househillmuir Primary School

MY BIRTHDAY

Today it is
My birthday
I got
A pair of skates
Clothes
Bobbles
Two Steps CDs
And I got
A doll but
It is an
Ornament
I got thirty pounds
I enjoyed it!

Louise Greenaway (10)
Househillmuir Primary School

THE FINAL

Rangers
Might play Celtic
In the final at
Hampden.
First time a game
Has been played there
Since it has been rebuilt.

Natasha Picken (10)
Househillmuir Primary School

A BIN

Your admirable smell,
I pray to you like a god.
Whenever I feel hungry,
I search inside of you.
Overnight drumsticks,
Leftover fish cake,
Outdated chocolate bars,
Unfinished crisps in the packet,
Whatever I need, it can be found in you.
A broken gear,
Dried up gluesticks,
Empty tins and bottles,
Ripped tin foils and wrappings,
Your admirable junk,
I find my treasure in you.

Joe Lau (10)
Kelvindale Primary School

ODE TO MY BIN

My bin, my bin, it's a weird shade of green,
It was supplied for me by the council and the Queen.
I got it in the year of 1993,
It was manufactured especially for me.
The opening of the lid sings a nice wee song,
And the smell that comes out is an obnoxious pong.
'That odour bin' I hear my mum say,
But I'll always love it night and day.

Andrew Duke (10)
Kelvindale Primary School

THE BUTTERFLY

It is such an amazing creature,
Simply from a caterpillar to red rouge wings.
The colours of the wings are like 10 rainbows,
There are even white wedding wings like snow,
The beautiful creature that Mother Nature makes.
It is a friend of the flowers,
The grasshoppers are astounded by its charm.
The weeds toil and bow at it as it flies past.
The cat plays with it all afternoon,
The wind spreads its beauty,
Till the dark moonlight shines on its wings.

Pooja Varyani (10)
Kelvindale Primary School

A CAT

Little miaows and purrs
Rubbing against your leg
When they see the food bowl
Being filled with something tasty
Tails start flickering
Eyes get wider
When the bowl touches the floor
Back arches up
Now the tongue starts licking
And they're only interested in what's in the bowl.

Jane Duncan (10)
Kelvindale Primary School

SEASHORE

Kids laughing and playing on the sand,
While lazy adults lie on mats and deckchairs,
In the sun, or under pretty parasols,
Done in all the colours of the rainbow - and more.
As the sun glints off lots of cameras,
People look for relief, by slurping ice-creams,
But most of it drips on the golden sand.
Then the sea comes trickling in,
And washes it away,
While further along the beach,
It crashes onto rocks, and fills up rockpools,
Calm, yet they sparkle in the sun,
Showing off their pretty fish,
Lobsters, crabs and jellyfish.
I uncover a rock, and they scuttle away,
While the jellyfish quiver.
I long to stay the rest of the day,
But we've got to go,
Away from the brightly-coloured swimmers,
Back home.

Clare Sutherland (10)
Kelvindale Primary School

THE SEASHORE

Pebbles are shining, glinting in the sun.
Children are running in and out of the waves, and splashing everyone.
Ice-cream dripping and it's sticky on your hand.
Sun is shining brightly, but I got burnt.
Waves are crashing, the tide is coming in and it is time to go home.

Shona Macmillan (10)
Kelvindale Primary School

CAT

Mice daren't go near it, a quick killer,
Their claws are like swords.
Its miaow puts happiness into my heart,
Its horse legs make it agile
As it runs across the floor,
Turning at acute angles.
A cheetah as it climbs trees,
A lion as it attacks the sparrows.
With its needle-sharp eyes it spots the enemy
As it barks like a foghorn.
Like a Ferrari, it speeds up the stairs.

Thomas Sutcliffe-Campo (11)
Kelvindale Primary School

SEASHORE

Kids splashing in the sea,
Ice-cream van rings, all the kids go running.
Children finding shells,
More people turning up with buckets and spades.
Mums and dads running.
Picnic baskets get opened,
Sun shining on the sand.

Jennifer McCann (11)
Kelvindale Primary School

IN MY HEAD

In my head live vampires
and zombies roaming free,
with evil dreams
and with warriors roaming killing all known hope.

In my head there are dreams
of love and death
shattered in life
and with love there comes hate and dreaded death,
caused by love and caring death.

In my head love and hate
come together in life
or in death
don't explain the hate in the world today.

Laura Gray (11)
Kelvindale Primary School

A FROG

A bouncy ball
A bug-eater
A lily-leaper
A gooey piece of slime
A silly animal
A water lover
A smelly animal.

Jason McMullen (10)
Kelvindale Primary School

THE ANTEATER

He has got giant claws
He uses as excavators.
Once he has made a hole
He launches an attack on the ants.
Like a tank, he sends a missile
Which is his extremely long tongue.
Bending round corners and catching ants.
His head rolls his tongue back into his mouth
Like a conveyor belt with dead ants on it.
Another victory is his.

Sean Stephen (10)
Kelvindale Primary School

ODE TO A TIN

Oh tin, how I envy you
Your shimmering metal body
With your gorgeous lid
To keep my money safe inside
You fall on my dad's toes
To stop him from getting my money
You may have a handsome label
With a picture of anything
Cats, pigs, gardens, anything
But my favourite is an animal.

Gillian Allan (10)
Kelvindale Primary School

DARK NIGHT

I've had a great time at my friends house,
Now it's time to go.
I exit through the back door
and into a spooky alley.
I wave farewell and walk down the cobble lane,
The door closes and it's time to go.
I feel scared and alone as I walk down the alley.

I hear dustbins turning over,
I hear cars in the distance,
I hear TVs blaring away.

As I walk down the cobble stone lane,
I see the strangest things,
I see dogs rolling about in bins,
I see cats jumping from wall to wall,
I even see, see wait a minute what's that.
      Argggh!

Iain O'Donnell (9)
Kelvindale Primary School

SKY

Relaxing blue
Thunder-maker
White picture
Night-maker
High sea
Sea of white fish
Birds' home.

James Sharp (10)
Kelvindale Primary School

ODE TO MY BRAIN

Oh brain, brain you are so exceptionally magnificent
And where would I be without you
To give me those impressive suggestions
To tell the teacher
So I could be star pupil
And if I didn't have you
I would be the dumbest in the class
So please don't ever jump out my head.

Leah Stevenson (10)
Kelvindale Primary School

ODE TO A SEAGULL

Oh, seagull, how tremendously useful you are
I love the way you take my sandwiches,
Especially when I don't like them.
It's great when you make a marvellous noise,
When I'm at school, so I don't have to listen,
I adore the way you remind me of the beach,
And get rid of the crabs,
That nip my toes in the sea
I marvel at the way you steal my sister's biscuit,
I think you're great.

Rebecca Drummond (10)
Kelvindale Primary School

My School Poem!

School is a place for working,
Everyone trying hard!
Some people are playing and fiddling,
With pencils, paper or card.

Desks are always dirty,
Especially always mine!
We're supposed to get out at half past three,
But we never get out on time!

Rachel Buckley (9)
Kelvindale Primary School

My Cat Smudge

My cat Smudge
Likes to play
He likes to
Play all day
But sometimes
He likes to sleep
He likes to
Sleep all day.

Emma Makan (9)
Kelvindale Primary School

SUMMER

Summer is coming back
The rain is still in
Bed.

Summer is getting hot
The rain is getting
Sad.

Sun shining
I felt like going
Swimming.

Tanya Kaur (9)
Kelvindale Primary School

SUN'S BACK

The sun is back
The rain's getting the sack
The summer's getting hired
The winter's getting fired
The snow is melting
The rain isn't pelting

So I'm glad
Yes glad
I'm not sad.

Vincent Okine (9)
Kelvindale Primary School

A CASTLE

The castle on the hill
A fortress strong and true
Who lived and fought for me

The castle on the hill
The dungeons dark and spooky
Who lived and fought for me

The castle on the hill
The black cannons sitting there
Who lived and fought for me

The castle on the hill
With a view of the sea
Who lived and fought for me

The castle on the hill
A fortress strong and true
Who lived and fought for me.

Lyndsay Dolan (9)
Kelvindale Primary School

I LOVE PLAYING FOOTBALL

I love playing football,
I love it when I get muddy in the park,
It's the best sport on earth.
I don't know what I'd do without it,
I love it when I score a goal,
Oh I do love football.

Garry McFarlane (9)
Kelvindale Primary School

I Just Love Talking

In school
I always talk.
People say I'm a
chatterbox.
The teacher says
Be quiet! Be quiet!
But somehow
I just can't stop.
I talk to
Anyone,
Anything,
Anywhere.
I suppose
I just love talking.

Jaskarn Khaira (9)
Kelvindale Primary School

My Gran

My gran she passed,
My gran she was fun,
My gran she gave me sweets,
My gran I miss,
My gran she was the best,
My gran I miss so so much,
My gran I want back.

Nicola Hunter (9)
Kelvindale Primary School

BEING ON YOUR OWN

I'm being kept inside,
Inside all day.
I'm all alone,
Alone in the house.
My heart has left my body,
My heart has gone away.

I'm coming back,
Like a new person.
I will go outside,
Outside to play.
But I'm still alone,
In a nice safe place.

Lewis Campbell (9)
Kelvindale Primary School

SPRING DAYS

Today it is sunny
And the sky is blue
The birds are singing
And chirping too.

Old leaves are falling
New leaves are growing
Together it makes
The whole wide world.

Stephanie Gray (9)
Kelvindale Primary School

THE MOON

I have always
wondered
wondered about the moon.

I have always wondered
if the craters are
all holes.

I have always wondered
wondered about
the moon
whether there
is life on it
like there is
on Earth.

I have always wondered
wondered about the
moon.

Euan Maharg (9)
Kelvindale Primary School

BOOKS

I like reading books,
Instead of television.
Flashing through all
the pages,
Taking in all the
information.

Victoria Hay (9)
Kelvindale Primary School

SUMMER

Summer is fun!
Summer is fun!
Out comes the big yellow sun
Everyone is out to play
In the hot summer days
Having picnics in the park
Dogs playing as they bark.

Summer is fun!
Summer is fun!
Down goes the big yellow sun.
Everyone goes home
Wishing they would go to Rome.
While at home time for bed
So it's off to sleep with baby Fred.

Summer is fun!
Summer is fun!

Ruth Grace McKay (10)
Kelvindale Primary School

SHADOWS

Alone in the dark
The shadows are coming to get me.
Alone in bed
Can't get to sleep.

Alone in the dark
The shadows are following me.
Alone in bed
Can't get to sleep.

Alone in the dark
The shadows are in my bed.
Alone in bed
Can't get to sleep.

Alone in the dark
The shadows don't scare me.
Alone in bed
Yes I am asleep.

Laura Porteous (9)
Kelvindale Primary School

SEASONS

Time for spring
The lambs all sing
Time for spring
What will summer bring?

It's summer now,
The sun comes out
Flowers grow
Their heads pop out.

It's autumn now,
The leaves all fall.
They fall from the trees
Yes the trees up tall.

Now it's winter, it's
Going all cold.
You better watch out
Or you will get a cold!

Michael Greenshields (9)
Kelvindale Primary School

TIGERS

Tigers are beautiful animals
With their orange and black stripes
It is beautiful to watch
Them hunt and lay around.

But people are shooting them
And chopping them up
They skin them
And sell the skins
The tigers did nothing
To them
So they should not
Be poached.

Emily H Waddell (9)
Kelvindale Primary School

LIFE

Life
Sometimes it's easy
Sometimes it's hard
Life can be fun.
You don't always
Get what you want
But sometimes you do.

People die
People live
But
I think life might
be fun.

Seonaid Weightman (9)
Kelvindale Primary School

THE WINDY WIND

Have you heard the wind
Whistling in the trees
When it is there,
There is a very big breeze
White clouds, grey clouds hurry by
So when they have gone there is
A clear blue sky.

Have you seen the wind
Blowing leaves about
The wind is weaving in the trees
Blowing more leaves off,
To carry in the breeze
Over the house and then the hills
Then over the golden daffodils
So far away I think it will
Be back another day.

Pamela Proctor (9)
Kelvindale Primary School

CAGED

I'm in a cage
Me by myself, all alone
I wish I was free
In my house, with my family.

But I'm all alone, in a cage,
Like a pet, by itself.
I feel like an overgrown budgie,
Locked up,
By itself,
All alone,
I'm lonely.

Gavia Baker Whitelaw (9)
Kelvindale Primary School

BULLIES

Bullies here they come
Thump, thump
Goes my heart
Run I think to myself
I try to run
But they've surrounded me
Thump, thump
I close my eyes
Here it comes
Aaaa Aaaa

Sarah Morgan (9)
Kelvindale Primary School

LITTLE PUPPY

Dear little puppy
How are you?
I'd like you to stay
to stay
to stay with me
right now.

Dear little puppy
How are you?
I'd like you to go
to go
to go with me
right now.

Emma Harkess (9)
Kelvindale Primary School

PLAYTIME

The bell rings
It's playtime the teacher says
Get your coats and line up
We run down the stairs
We play all sorts of things
Like hide and seek and farmer, farmer
Then the bell rings, ring, ring
Bye we say to our friends
And then we line up.

Alexandra Mellon (9)
Kelvindale Primary School

NIGHT-TIME BATS

I wish I could be as free as a bat
Flying about at night.
It does not get told what to do
You can have a mind of your own.

Oh I wish I could be a bat,
I'm so helpless and so shy,
Oh I wish I could be a bat only going out at
Night.

Victoria Trotter (9)
Kelvindale Primary School

THE SUNSHINE DAY

The bright sun breaks through,
As the dark clouds leave the sky.
It's like a dream come true,
As the birds they fly.

I can feel the hotness against me,
As it is scorching down on earth.
When the children play at sea,
It's probably very hot in Perth.

Night has come, it has cooled down,
The light of the moon has arrived.
It is silent in the town.
I'll wake up to another sunshine day.

Katrina Raine (11)
Kilbowie Primary School

THE TITANIC

It was a night in September
But as warm as June.
The ship was sailing calmly,
There was a full glowing moon.

The boat was going fast,
The iceberg was coming near.
Then the Titanic hit it,
And there were sights of fear.

This day was tragic,
The story is not pretend.
Not everybody survived,
As the boat came to an end.

Samantha Harden (11)
Kilbowie Primary School

MY FAVOURITE ANIMAL

There are so many animals so lovely to see,
But only one is right for me,
Some are cute and some are bold,
But most of them have a heart of gold,
People treat them bad,
And I think cruelty is very sad,
But my favourite animal can be big or wee,
It's the one that wags it tail and runs to me.

Stacey Paterson (10)
Kilbowie Primary School

SUMMER DIES

Summer dies,
But don't sigh,
Why winter is here.

Bears, birds and hedgehogs,
Migrate and hibernate,
But there's still one person who stays.

Mr Robin red breast,
And we can't forget Jack Frost,
When we hear the golden crunch of
leaves,
And sparkling frost on cars.

Billy Cameron (9)
Lairdsland Primary School

AUTUMN

Leaves of golden brown are falling down,
Some people playing,
Some people praying,
Summer is dying, dying,
Autumn is coming, coming.

Snow is down, no playground,
Birds are away,
Robins come out to play,
Animals are tucked away safe and warm.

William Murray (9)
Lairdsland Primary School

DEAD SUMMER

The air is cold the wind is strong,
The sun has faded,
The flowers are dead,
The leaves have fallen,
Winter is here, is here, is here.

The snow is soft,
The sharp, ruby red berries are here,
Upon the treetops
There is snow, there is snow.

Summer is dying, dying, dying,
Summer . . . has gone.

Emma Glen (9)
Lairdsland Primary School

AUTUMN IS COMING

On the last summer night,
The cricket sang his summer song,
As the night sky turned black,
He said to himself,
Summer is dying and autumn is coming,
Summer is dying and autumn is coming.
As he sang his song his feet tapped
together,
Tap, tap, that made a sort of chilling sound.

Sam Gilmour (9)
Lairdsland Primary School

THE HEDGEHOG AND ROBIN

I am a hedgehog,
When the leaves fall,
And the ground turns cold,
I hide away and sleep.

I am a robin,
When the frost comes,
And the wind is cold,
I puff my feathers up to keep warm.

Lauren Horner (9)
Lairdsland Primary School

THE END OF SUMMER

At the end of summer,
The animals hibernate,
Birds fly away to other countries,
The weather gets colder and colder.

Leaves lay on the ground,
And we can throw them about,
At the end of winter,
A new year will come.

Ben Stirling (9)
Lairdsland Primary School

THE END OF SUMMER

Leaves falling off trees,
Shorter days, colder days,
A bear sleeping,
But where?
Somewhere in the winter woods.

Birds migrate south,
Shorter days, colder days,
In trees squirrels are storing,
But what?
A store of nuts and berries.

A robin comes to see me,
In the winter days.
He comes and speaks to me,
He has to search for food,
And then he flies away.

Colin MacDougall (9)
Lairdsland Primary School

SUMMER IS AT AN END

Summer is going,
        Summer is going,
                Back to school we go.

The days now grow short,
        And golden brown leaves
                Fall off the trees.

Karen Gordon (9)
Lairdsland Primary School

THE DRAGON

A shepherd boy stares at the sky as a
vast shadow appears.
It starts to swoop down and becomes
very near,
Half fearful, half entranced,
In the sun its scales seem to dance.
Its long neck weaved and arched like a snake
Its wings were sharp, spiked and ready to break.
The shepherd watched despite his fear,
But luckily it didn't come very near.

Iain Boot (9)
Lairdsland Primary School

SUMMER IS COMING TO AN END

Today the trees are growing bare,
The leaves are falling to the ground,
And the sky is cold and grey.

Today the animals hibernate,
Conkers fall to the ground,
Now summer's dead and gone.

Karen Beresford (9)
Lairdsland Primary School

THE DRAGON

With eyes of red and sapphire head,
the dragon wheeled round the sun,
with a body encrusted with jewels that,
are dusted with smoke that encircled
the air.

Its long purple neck waved and arched
like a snake moving round through
the sand.
Sharp, pointed wings stooping,
it came to get closer to land,
then gobbled up my fattest ram.

Stephanie Holbein
Lairdsland Primary School

DRAGON

Its jewel encrusted head soared
against the sun,
Its long neck waved,
and arched like a snake's
Its wings were sharp
spiked and tipped with
sapphires, diamonds and pearls
Its sharp talons stuck into
the back of the fattest ram.

Calvin Wilson (9)
Lairdsland Primary School

UNDER THE SEA

Under the sea is everyone's dream,
Under the sea for you and me.
The sea, the beautiful sea.
The sea is there today and tomorrow,
The sea is there for you to sorrow.
The sea, the beautiful sea.
Toss a coin into the sea,
See the ripples and be free.
The sea, the beautiful sea.

Nicole Anne Welsh (8)
Lamlash Primary School

UP IN SPACE

Up in space
there are many planets.
Some have got funny names
like Jupiter, Neptune and Mercury.

Up in space
it is very dark.
There are planets
like Mars
which sounds like a
Mars bar.

John McIver (9)
Lamlash Primary School

THE THINGS I LIKE

I like feeling the summer breeze,
Also eating the Easter eggs.
Through the summer I go out
to stay with my friends it is great.
When the summer ends, next up
is Christmas.
I'll get all my presents on the day.
The month after the happy new year!

These are the things I like.

Steven McCarter (8)
Lamlash Primary School

THE WORLD IS ROUND

The world is round, the world is round,
But why is the world round?
Could it be square or triangle,
But why is the world round, no one knows?
A little boy didn't know, his mum didn't know,
        But who knows then?

Pamela Stewart (8)
Lamlash Primary School

HURRAH THE MILLENNIUM'S COME

Bing bong goes the clock,
Ding dong the bells are here.
Hurrah! The millennium's come.
Crazy children celebrating,
Men, as mad as March hares,
Women waving frantically,
Hurrah! The millennium's come.
Kisses, cuddles everywhere,
Celebrating all around the world,
Hurrah! The millennium's come.
Singers singing madly,
A pipe band heard through the streets,
Hurrah! The millennium's come.
Shouting, laughing, cries for joy,
People getting drunk,
Hurrah! The millennium's come.

Catherine Gillies (11)
Our Lady Of The Missions Primary School

CELEBRATION TIME

Maybe next millennium,
We won't have to go out,
To celebrate the new beginning,
Year 3000 there they go!

But what about today, though,
When the clock strikes twelve,
Will you be going out?
If you are, good luck!

It must be quite a fight, though,
Getting through the crowds.
Grab your new year cheer,
2000 here we come!

Mary-Clare Friel (11)
Our Lady Of The Missions Primary School

CELEBRATION 2000

The next millennium
Is approaching fast.
Celebrations start at last.
Years and years of shouts and cheers,
Are brought together after 1000 years.

But will our millennium be a peaceful one,
Or will there be the same old scum?
Will the poor be poorer,
Or will we hear their call?

Our daily inventions will soon make way,
For better ones on this new day.
Buses, cars will be remade,
And it could be robots who get paid.

Our past millennium,
Was it good?
Do we need a better, cleaner, more peaceful
World?
I think we do.
What about you?

Brendan McKenna (11)
Our Lady Of The Missions Primary School

CELEBRATING 2000

As the days go passing by,
This millennium is saying goodbye,
Everybody it will excite,
And because of the occasion
I'll say, 'Quite right!'
With all the new inventions coming soon,
Let's hope to have our holidays on the moon.
Will there be a flying car,
Or will there be a planet not very far?
Will a jungle be in my back yard,
Or will there be a species made of card?
Will dinosaurs come back to life,
Or will the president be my uncle,
Cameron Fyfe?
If all these crazy things come true,
Will they be strange to me or you?

Connell Duffy (11)
Our Lady Of The Missions Primary School

MILLENNIUM PEACE

Today tomorrow there will be no sorrow, for the millennium
is coming near, peace no war, love and no hatred.

Today tomorrow there will be no sorrow for the millennium
is coming near.
Why do you fight? Why don't you love?
There will be a year of peace.

In the future I think there will be a real peace because
people will come to their senses, but for today we pray
and hope there will be no war or fighting.

I wish you peace and joy for the future and for the well-being
of your families.

Eamonn Farrell (11)
Our Lady Of The Missions Primary School

MILLENNIUM FEVER

It's the new dawn of a thousand years,
laughs and shouts and screams and cheers.
Only sixty seconds until everyone will be jumping
with thrill.
Faces will widen with smiles of joy,
great atmosphere surrounding every girl and boy.
Thirty seconds pass right by,
but another soon arrive.
The clock ticks away and the excitement builds fast,
hoping midnight will come at last.
'Ten, nine, eight, seven, six,'
everyone shouts as the clock ticks and ticks.
'Five, four, three, two,' everybody blares,
people do some crazy things and no one really
cares.
Then that final time has come when everyone
screams that number *one!*

Jade Corral (11)
Our Lady Of The Missions Primary School

THE MILLENNIUM

Is the millennium coming?
Oh yes it will come
With a tremendous cheer,
Next year.

The millennium will come,
With a big round face,
To end the year with
A happy cheer.

With amazement we'll watch
The firework display,
Since it's better now
It's the millennium.

The riots in the street,
Caused by drunken men,
Will cause mayhem
On the roads,
For dancing parades.

As we watch the countdown
We'll build up our cheer
So when the clock strikes twelve
We'll give the biggest cheer
Ever.

And we'll shout out to the world
Happy New Year!

Laura Jane Casserly (11)
Our Lady Of The Missions Primary School

MILLENNIUM POEM

In the millennium
will man's heart be loving and caring,
instead of stale and selfish?
Maybe, just maybe.

In the millennium
will waters be blue and clear,
instead of dull and polluted?
Maybe, just maybe.

In the millennium
will wild animals run freely about their habitat,
instead of dead animals
lying in a place that was once
a place to call home?
Maybe, just maybe.

In the millennium
will the air we breathe be invigorating and fresh,
instead of car fumes ruining our planet?
Maybe, just maybe.

In the millennium
will the rainforests all across the world
have miles of green treetops,
instead of hearing the shrill cry of trees
at the point of the woodcutter's axe?
Maybe, just maybe.

Most importantly,
will the year 2000 be the year of justice
and peace throughout the planet?
Maybe, just maybe.

Julie Hunter (11)
Our Lady Of The Missions Primary School

MILLENNIUM

Fun will it be when the clock strikes twelve,
The parties kick off, fun to see,
We will enjoy this millennium just wait and see.

The day it comes I'll dance with glee,
Edinburgh's the place to be.

The millennium parties will be a blast,
They won't be forgotten when they've passed.

Millennium, millennium will be here at last,
Only a while to go
Till the millennium, you know.
It'll be here at last -
Not faded in the past.

Millennium will be here,
So give a cheer!

Mark Lyons (11)
Our Lady Of The Missions Primary School

CELEBRATION 2000

In the millennium,
We'll have cars that can fly,
With people hovering by.
The news will spread,
Like butter on bread,
Because the millennium has come.

In the millennium,
We'll all have a laser gun,
And a different meaning of fun.
We'll have different games,
And better names,
Because the millennium has come.

In the millennium,
People will cry,
'The end is nigh!'
With solar powered boats,
Tested across moats,
Because the millennium has come.

Iain Carnegie (11)
Our Lady Of The Missions Primary School

HAPPY NEW MILLENNIUM

The clock strikes twelve,
Hip hip hooray!
The new *millennium* has arrived today.

Everyone shouts, 'Happy new year!'
The whole world lets out an enormous
Big cheer.

The champagne is opened,
While the bells ring out,
And everyone cheers,
Hear people shout,
'Happy new year!'

The new generation is coming your way,
And everyone will come out to play,
They'll party,
They'll laugh,
They'll scream and they'll shout,
And plenty of people will be moving about.

A thousand years have finally passed,
The new *millennium* is here at last.

Stephanie Boyle (11)
Our Lady Of The Missions Primary School

MILLENNIUM

2000 years I can't wait,
Lots of food upon my plate.
I hope I'm not late,
Me and my mate.
The Millennium Bug might be a hug
Or might be a mug.
Celebrations and parties
And lots of Smarties.
Cake and food
I know it will be good.

Lisa Dragoonis (12)
Our Lady Of The Missions Primary School

FIREWORKS

Bright colours fill the sky,
Children merry standing by,
Rockets whizzing up above,
Like a shining flashing star.
People watching, people stare
Brightness fills their glare.
Fireworks whistling above our heads,
Fireworks lighting up the sky.

John Hendrie (11)
Oxgang Primary School

FIREWORKS

Flashing colours fill the sky
Into the air they go bye bye
Red, blue and green rockets go whooshing into the air
Everyone's here to see the fireworks at the fair
Whistling and howling is all you can hear
Of all things here each year
This is the one that hurts your ear
Rushing over your head are rockets
Kids are scared
Their eyes out of their sockets
Sizzling loud the Catherine wheels
       That's fireworks!

James Wright (11)
Oxgang Primary School

WINTER

It is winter and wind is howling,
it makes me shiver when it blows.
The air is chilly and nippy.
Small flakes of snow are falling on
the damp ground.
It is freezing.

Louise Neilson (11)
Oxgang Primary School

ZOOMING

Zoom, whiz, boom wow.
Over there astonishing rockets glide into the night
Over the buildings up and boom, technicoloured stars
Mum says, 'It's a Catherine wheel.'
Into the sky fly these magnificent spiralling fireballs.
Now it's all over, but . . . wait a minute . . .
            Boom!
Golden lightning zooms up to space.

Stuart McGaw (11)
Oxgang Primary School

RAIN

Damp
Wet
Drench
Pouring
Showers of rain
Bucketing
Raining cats and dogs
The heavens have opened.

Christopher Connell (11)
Oxgang Primary School

CELEBRATION 2000

M is for millennium in the new year
I   is for invitation
L is for love
L is for learning
E is for evolution
N is for new year
N is for neighbours
I   is for interesting
U is for unbelievable
M is for *millennium.*

Christopher Stewart (10)
Rogerfield Primary School

EASTER SUNDAY

On Easter Sunday
my mum hides my eggs
I have to look and look and look
before I get to eat them
and when I find them
I get to eat them
and when I eat and eat them up
I always get full up.

Sarah Allison (9)
Rogerfield Primary School

THE BEAUTIFUL BIRD

One day I saw a blue bird
Flying in the sky
It was there when I saw it
From my window
I said
What a beautiful bird.

I went to see the bird
But it flew away.

Karen McFarlane (9)
Rogerfield Primary School

RAINBOW BIRD

There it was flying in the skies
A beautiful bird before my eyes
Many colours for me to see
I saw it while eating my tea
My eyes popped out
And my mouth couldn't shout
It was a rainbow bird of course.

Kayleigh Baldwin (9)
Rogerfield Primary School

EASTER

When winter comes
You're happy
But trees are sad
With snow

Easter is a happy time
When trees and flowers grow
But when you see the winter
You think it'll never go.

John William Dickson (9)
Rogerfield Primary School

CELEBRATION 2000

M illennium Dome, party 2000!
I   nvitation to a millennium party.
L oud party animals,
L oud fireworks in Edinburgh.
E ntertainment groups,
N oisy crowd having a good time.
N ot a lot of sleep for anyone!
I   nside parties, inside and out.
M illennium celebrations in every house.

Kevin Paterson (10)
Rogerfield Primary School

CELEBRATION 2000

M illennium is the year 2000
I t is a new year celebration
L ove everyone in your family -
L ove all your friends
E njoy the year 2000
N ew year is a very nice time
N ew century even better
I t is a time to celebrate
U nder the mistletoe people get kissed
M illennium dome 2000.

Amanda Palmer (10)
Rogerfield Primary School

MILLENNIUM

M illennium
I s a new century
L ights going on everywhere
L ighter than the moon
E verybody's happy -
N ot at eleven but at twelve.
N ow is the hour
I n every country.
U mbrellas if it's raining - that will not stop the celebration
M any shouting and cheering at the celebration.

Marc Hendry (10)
Rogerfield Primary School

CELEBRATION 2000

M illennium celebration!
I nvitation
L oud people
L oud noise
E xcitement
N ervous
N oisy
I nside party
U nlimited fun
M illennium celebration!

Jonathan Daly (11)
Rogerfield Primary School

CELEBRATION 2000

Imagine at the millennium
A brand new century.
The bells will ring at 12 o'clock
Everyone will get up and say 'Happy new year'
Celebrate a new century.
Have a drink to celebrate the new year.
Wake up the next morning in a different century.

David McClung (10)
Rogerfield Primary School

CELEBRATION 2000

M idnight
I n your house.
L ights are on.
L onging for the doorbell to ring.
E njoy the night.
N o other nights will be the same!
N oisy neighbours in the street.
I n the house, I sit and wonder,
U sing candles through the night, only for
M illennium night.

Scott Docherty (10)
Rogerfield Primary School

CHARLENE AND THE QUEEN

There once was a girl called Charlene
Who lived up in Aberdeen
She went to a dance
'Cos she had the chance
To meet the queen Irene.

David Molloy (10)
Rogerfield Primary School

CELEBRATION 2000

As the new millennium dawns,
we think of history.
Dinosaurs are gone, no more
stamping on the ground.
No longer living in black old
dirty caves.
Feather quills are gone and pencils
are here!

1999 and life is very different!
Keyhole surgery has healed all pain.
Food processors crushing all the food.
Satellites watching TV programmes
from all over the world.
Big rockets taking you up to space.

The next millennium?
What will it bring?
Medicines! Magic! Take away your pain
Time travel will take me to the days
of dinosaurs again.
Food of the future?
Banana tablets!
Playing will be different,
we'll play with helter-skelter skates
which float down hills.

Stacey McCreadie (8)
St Aloysius' Primary School, Springburn

CELEBRATION 2000

As the new millennium dawns
We think of history.
Like wagons screeching and noisy gallops coming by
People used to live in lighthouses.
Flashing the bright light telling boats of pointy
rocks ahead
Dinosaurs crashing through the jungle
Crushing all the plants.

1999 and life is very different
Because of the technology
People have instant food from McDonald's
Mums say they want cosmetic surgery!
You can use food processors
People like two sandwiches with a banana
Mrs McKeeve likes her dishwasher
Because it helps her with the dishes.

The next millennium?
What will it bring?
Yes there is pain with diseases going round.

My time travel will take me on a holiday
to the other side of the earth.

I would like to travel back in time to
see my gran.

I would not like tablets for dinner or
tea or snacks.
It will be fun if you want to go to
another world.

Sarah Jane Queen
St Aloysius' Primary School, Springburn

CELEBRATION 2000

As the new millennium dawns
We think of history.
We do not have dinosaurs,
They are extinct, along with the mammoth
We do not have slate fires anymore.
We do not have feather quills to write with.

1999 and life is very different
There are new inventions.
Mobile phones to communicate.
We have a satellite TV.
We listen to music.
You can use a washing machine.
You only have to sit down,
Wait for the washing machine to stop.
You can taste other food,
From other countries.

The next millennium!
What will it bring?
All of the pain will go away.
Someone will make new medicines,
The pain will disappear.
Time travel! A little case!
Press a little button and you're off.

What will you eat?
You will eat tablets and vitamins.
You can be healthy.
It will be brilliant!
You will have new toys.
Supersonic skates and supersonic skateboards.

Jason Bird (8)
St Aloysius' Primary School, Springburn

CELEBRATION 2000

As the new millennium dawns
We think of history.
No dinosaurs roaming our planet.
Vikings no longer rob us.
Our clothes are not made of animal skins.
We no longer have feather quills,
We do not have to walk everywhere.
Do-dos and mammoths no longer exist.

1999 and life is very different!
We now have submarines to explore the sea bed.
Combine harvesters, space travel to the moon
And other planets like Pluto and Mars.
Foreign holidays and technology!
Computers, dishwashers, microscopes
To see all different things that other people can't,
Exotic fruits like mangoes, kiwi fruit, pineapples,
Coconuts, bananas,
Machines for food, food processors,
No longer have we to get cut open thanks to
Keyhole surgery.

The next millennium?
What will it bring?
Pain is like getting knocked down
But the technology will come for this planet of death.

My time travel will take me to a country
Of peace and love.
No death, no murder, no wars - just peace and love.

Food will be tablets, pills and capsules.
Drink with vitamins - no sugar.

Fun will be computers - no more school
And no work or teachers or head teachers!

Christopher Maguire (8)
St Aloysius' Primary School, Springburn

CELEBRATION 2000

As the new millennium dawns,
We think of history.
We don't have caves and cave men to kill animals to eat.
We don't have dinosaurs to eat other animals.
No horses to take us to other countries.
We don't have black and white TV, colour and satellite rule!
Romans and Vikings don't invade our country and destroy the lands.

1999, and life is very different!
We have phones and central heating in our houses,
Machines to do our work,
We have space rockets to go to space,
Trains to take us somewhere at fast speed.

The next millennium!
What will it bring?
Pain is not going to exist!
We'll have tablets and medicine to cure death and infection.
Travel back into when Jesus was alive.
The food of the future in a thousand years,
Tablets and medicine with vitamins.
Fun swimming in pools and fun with computers.
The next millennium will be magic!

Helena Martha Walker (8)
St Aloysius' Primary School, Springburn

CELEBRATION 2000

As the new millennium dawns
We think of history.
(We don't have to travel by big, creaking wagons).
We don't have damp, cold caves.
We don't have big horses and carts,
Dinosaurs, prehistoric reptiles lived in damp, cold caves.

1999, and life is very different!
Now we can go to MacDonald's
We can go out for a meal.
We can visit nice shops to buy beautiful clothes.
Now we have foreign holidays.

We have new money and new notes.
We have new computers.
We now have all different kinds of machines.
Now people can work all around the world.

The next millennium!
What will it bring?

We will get medicine to keep us well.
In time travel we can press a button
And we would be in another world.
For food we would have tablets for our dinner.
For fun we could play with supersonic skates.

Angela Doherty (8)
St Aloysius' Primary School, Springburn

CELEBRATION 2000

As the new millennium dawns,
We think of history.
Feather quills have been replaced by pens and pencils.
No longer do we rub sticks to make fires.
We don't ride on horses anymore.
We now have aeroplanes and cars.
No longer do we live in draughty, old, grey caves.

1999 and life is very different!
We can travel to space in rockets,
Go on foreign trips to lots of hot countries.
We have lots of magic washing machines,
They wash all your clothes,
No more going to the river anymore.
Lots of juicy, exotic fruits,
Pineapples and coconuts.
Lots of instant food as well,
Curries and long spaghetti.

The next millennium!
What will it bring?
We will have magic cures.
People coming back to life as well.
You won't need to go to the doctor to cure pain.
You just have to go to the shops,
Buy a special cure and drink it.

I will have magic skates
Tell them where I want to go.
We will eat special pieces of chewing gum
That tastes like a starter, then a main meal and then a desert.
We will play with skates that can jump.

Gillian Skinner (8)
St Aloysius' Primary School, Springburn

CELEBRATION 2000

As the new millennium dawns, think of history,
like dinosaurs all banging around the earth.
People on wagons, thumping and squeaking
from place to place and waking everybody up.
People taking feathers of birds and using them for feather quills.
Women using scrubbing boards to wash their clothes.
Black and white television that men and women used to watch.

1999 and life is very different!

We can use dish washers instead of washing your dishes yourself.
We have got MacDonald's with the Happy Meals.
Exotic fruits, like coconuts and bananas.

The next millennium, what will it bring?

There is not going to be pain in the next millennium.
We can help people who have diseases.
Make the world a happy place.
Time travel can take me to Orlando, Florida.
Going back in time to see the Egyptians

I think the next millennium will be fun.

Danielle Maguire (8)
St Aloysius' Primary School, Springburn

AAH!

My head hurts.
My life's in a mess.
I can't talk, I'm feeling the stress.
I don't know how and
I don't know why.
Sometime now I'm going to cry.

Tony Neil
St John's Primary School

MY EARTHLY GUARDIAN ANGEL

Things feel so wrong when you're gone,
My life feels upside down when you're not around,
When there's a fight or an argument, you blow the whistle,
You seem to simplify every obstacle.
When you're around things are never awkward,
Complicated or disorganised.
You give every last effort and every last care,
Which is why 'Don't ever leave me' is what I repeat in a prayer.

Your personality was one of a kind,
and I thought the love we shared would never unbind.
Unfortunately you couldn't maintain,
and you created an immense amount of pain.
The way we combined was extremely rare,
you were the only one I knew who could give me that care,
you turned your back and left me here,
and it was after that I realised that you were extremely sincere,
my heart sank when your generosity did die,
but the greatest sorrow of all, you didn't say goodbye.
My feelings for you, words cannot describe,
and although this is just a poem, it comes directly from inside,
as the years go by the memories fad,
but I'll never forget the bricks that you laid.

Christy McFadden
St John's Primary School

NOISES

Zoom! Goes a motorbike driving by.
Squeak! Squeak! goes a bicycle.
Crash! Goes an icicle falling down.
Chitter, chatter! goes the lady in her night-gown.
'Evening Times' says the man selling papers with a frown.
Loud music, where would be without it.
Wa! Wa! Goes a baby as if it fell in a pit.
Zoom! Squeak! Crash! Chitter, Evening Times
And a baby's cry.
These are sounds I hear going by.

Maureen McGarvey (11)
St John's Primary School

THE COMPUTER GAME

She loved the presents
But most of all
She loved the computer game
With a little dinosaur
With a little spiky back
Firing little balls
At the baddies
In moving bubbles
With little hens
And little bricks.

Jaclyn McMahon (8)
St Julie's Primary School, Glasgow

THE DOLLY

She loved the presents
But most of all
She loved the doll
With long blonde hair
Hanging down
Sitting on the beach
Sunning herself
And a hat
And suntan lotion
With a lovely swimming
costume.

Dionne Sloan (9)
St Julie's Primary School, Glasgow

THE PRAM

She loved the presents
but most of all
She loved the pram
With a rain cover
blue stripes
Covering the dolly
Rainy day
A white shawl
And a basket
And some round wheels.

Stephanie Cartwright (8)
St Julie's Primary School, Glasgow

THE DRESS

She loved the presents
But most of all
She loved the dress
With nice looking frills
Stitched on
That are flapping around
Windy day
And a zip
A striped pattern
And a pink stripe.

John McGinty (8)
St Julie's Primary School, Glasgow

THE BALL

I'm being carried to the game
Where the children aim to get my head straight in the goal!
They have to kick me with their toes,
If they miss it will be no fun but Heaven help,
I hope they won!
By now you'll know that I'm the ball, round and fat and not too tall!
As I sit on my spot, trembling with fear,
I realise the boy who kicks softly is out with a sore ear!

Amanda Donaghy (11)
St Julie's Primary School, Glasgow

A BALL'S LIFE

I'm a little football, not very tall.
They kick me with their toe just to see me go.
They try to put me in the goal but then just
hit me off the pole.
They always get into a mood, blaming me
because they're no good!
But at the next game they kiss me for luck,
What a life for a very small ball!

Stephanie McIntyre (11)
St Julie's Primary School, Glasgow

HAPPINESS

Happiness is going to see my baby cousin.
I was happy when I was drawing football players.
Happiness is eating my Hula Hoops.
I am happy when I am playing football with my pals.
Happiness is going down to the shops.
I was happy when I went to the swimming pool.
I am happy when I am climbing big trees.
Happiness is going to the ice rink.
I am happy when I play my Super Nintendo.
I was happy when I was building a den.
Happiness is riding on my bike.
I am happy when I am sliding about in the rain.

Craig Mochan (8)
St Leonard's Primary School, East Kilbride

HAPPINESS

Happiness is when my baby cousin was born.
Happiness is my mum's new car.
Happiness is when I got my guinea pigs.
I am happy when I watch TV.
Happiness is playing with my friends.
Happiness is when I go to church.
Happiness is my new school.
I am happy when I am eating ice-cream.
Happiness is my family and friends.
Happiness is a day at the seaside.
Happiness is burgers to eat.
Happiness is going on holiday.

Catriona Cameron (8)
St Leonard's Primary School, East Kilbride

EATING A SUN LOLLY

Happiness is eating a Sun Lolly
Happiness is when friends come to my house
I feel happy when I go to the park with my sister
I feel happy when I draw cats and owls
Happiness is when I'm at the Brownies
Happiness is when I go to the swimming pool
I feel happy when I watch Sooty and Co
I feel happy when I read the Top of the Pops magazine.

Anna Mulrain (7)
St Leonard's Primary School, East Kilbride

HAPPINESS

Happiness is when I play with my friends,
Happiness is when I lick my cola lollipop.
Happiness is when my mum makes a dinner on Sunday.
I was happy when I had a Snickers.
I was happy when I played the Nintendo 64.
Happiness is when I do my tap.
Happiness is when I have an ice-cream.
Happiness is when I play tig.
I was happy when I looked up the dictionary.
Happiness is when my friend comes in for me.

Katie Park (7)
St Leonard's Primary School, East Kilbride

HAPPINESS

Happiness is eating vanilla ice-cream.
I was happy going to Australia on holiday.
Happiness is my mum having a new baby in December.
Happiness is going swimming with my dad.
Happiness is doing mental maths and reading.
I was happy going in an aeroplane.
Happiness is going to the hospital because you get toys to play with.

Stephanie Tracey (8)
St Leonard's Primary School, East Kilbride

HAPPINESS

Happiness is eating ice-cream on a sunny day.
Happiness was my uncle winning £350.
Happiness is my birthday.
Happiness is going to the cinema with my friends.
Happiness is drinking orange juice on a very hot day.
Happiness is going swimming.
Happiness is going on a bike ride with my dad.
Happiness is when Christmas is here.
Happiness is going on holiday.
Happiness is going to school.
Happiness is playing outside on my rollerblades.
Happiness is doing PE.
Happiness is eating a juicy melon in summer.

Jennifer McKeown (8)
St Leonard's Primary School, East Kilbride

HAPPINESS

Happiness is getting my Scotland goalie top.
I am happy when I play my Super Nintendo.
Happiness is going out to play.
I am happy eating ice-cream.
Happiness is when I eat a flake.
Happiness was when my little sister was born.
Happiness was when I got my Super Nintendo games.

Adam Jackson (8)
St Leonard's Primary School, East Kilbride

HAPPINESS

Happiness is playing on a bouncy castle
I was happy when I was riding on my bike
Happiness is watching the acrobats at the circus
I was happy when I stayed up late to watch a film
Happiness is sleeping in on Saturday and Sunday
I was happy when I went to visit my cousins
Happiness is going to the zoo and seeing the birds
I was happy when I went on holiday to Flamingoland
Happiness is having a birthday party
I was happy when my dad got a new car
Happiness is going to a birthday party
I was happy when I had a Christmas dinner
Happiness is eating ice-cream
I was happy when I went to visit my gran.

Nicola Waddell (8)
St Leonard's Primary School, East Kilbride

I WILL PUT IN THE BOX

I will put in the box shapes
of all sizes from all over the world,
I will lock the winter cold air in the box.
I will trap up the fighting and let out the peace.
I will put in the darkness and let out the colours.
My box is made of colours and animals.

Collette Jarvie (10)
St Leonard's Primary School, East Kilbride

COLD SENSES

As I turn around I hear my footsteps
cracking the crisp snow.
I see my breath white and wispy
when I talk.
I taste my scarf warm and woolly.
Then I fall and feel the sharp
cold tingle of icy snow.
I stumble towards the house
and smell dinner's cooking
warm and welcoming.

Jacqueline Carroll (10)
St Leonard's Primary School, East Kilbride

HAPPINESS

Happiness is sitting in the sun.
Swimming in the swimming baths.
Happiness is writing.
I am happy playing inside with my friends.
Happiness is getting letters from my pen pal.
I am happy getting Christmas presents.
Happiness is going to school.
I am happy when I got my new kitten.
Happiness is New Year's Day.

Gemma Miller (7)
St Leonard's Primary School, East Kilbride

A Night-Time Poem

The wind whistles round
the room sending shivers
down my back,
Bringing in sounds,
owls hooting, trees rustling,
Then the shadows cast on the wall,
men creeping along,
strange animals lying everywhere you look
ready to pounce on you and take you away,
But then I think to myself
nothing's going to happen,
Then I drift off to sleep
into a silent world of dreams.

Linsay Waddell (10)
St Leonard's Primary School, East Kilbride

I Will Put In My Box

The darkest eeriest cave,
A small falling star crying
The tallest skyscraper
Full of gold all of mine
Saving it all for just one time
The smell of new cut wood.
That's what's in that box of mine.

Liam Farrell (10)
St Leonard's Primary School, East Kilbride

HAPPINESS

Happiness is playing the PC,
Happiness is getting a toy,
Happiness is going to my gran's,
Happiness is playing football,
Happiness is playing hockey,
Happiness is being on rollerblades,
Happiness is getting my room turned
                into a Scotland room,
Happiness is playing the Sony PlayStation,
Happiness is eating sweets,
Happiness is getting goalie gloves,
Happiness is going to sleep.

David Hart (7)
St Leonard's Primary School, East Kilbride

I WILL PUT IN THE BOX

I will put in the box
A silver surfer sailing slowly,
A shining bright star that's shot from the sky.
A fierce warrior waiting for an army to fight.
An ocean liner on a voyage.
My box has a cover made from sea shells
And is special to me.

John Paul Rafferty (10)
St Leonard's Primary School, East Kilbride

THE FROST

I see the ice lying on the open alleyway.
The wind whistling through the trees.
Though best of all is the taste of hot chocolate
Dripping down my throat.
I feel the frost nipping at my nose.
Worst of all I can smell the stinky exhaust
Coming from the cars.

Katrina Duncan (10)
St Leonard's Primary School, East Kilbride

EYES

My eyes are blue
Blue as the sea sparkling in the sun
With sparkling touches of white
White as snowflakes when they are falling from the sky
With sprinkles of black fading in
Black as the sky when it has just struck midnight
With tiny dabbles of green
Green as the freshly made leaves in the spring
And in the middle it is completely black with sparkles of white.

Karen Ferguson (9)
St Leonard's Primary School, East Kilbride

EYES

My eyes are blue
Blue as the sky in summer
Blue as the ocean on a mid summer's day
My eyes are speckled with light green
As green as fresh cut grass
As green as leaves in the summer
With jet black centres
Black as a blackbird's wing
Black as a panther moving silently.

Sinead Jackson (9)
St Leonard's Primary School, East Kilbride

EYES

My eyes are bright blue,
Blue as the blue sky
On a morning's day.
As blue as the sea sparkling on a hot day
With a touch of grey.
Grey as wet cement,
Specked with a touch of yellow.
Yellow as a daisy waving in the wind.

Katie Thomas (9)
St Leonard's Primary School, East Kilbride

EYES

My eyes are blue,
Blue as the rushing river on a summer's day.
They sparkle bright as a star in the day
With a hint of green,
Green as the green grass swaying
And as grey as the dark cloudy sky,
And sometimes they shine like sapphires
While I smile all day long.

Julianne Gallacher (10)
St Leonard's Primary School, East Kilbride

EYES

My eyes are dark brown.
Brown as a bear's fur, glossy and dark,
Brown as a tree bark,
Brown as shiny paint on a wall.
My eyes are dotted with black.
Black as a blackboard,
Black as a blackbird flying east,
Black as black ink spilling onto paper.

Douglas Kerr (9)
St Leonard's Primary School, East Kilbride

EYES

My eyes are blue,
As blue as the sea on a summer's day,
As blue as the daylight sky.
My eyes are like river rapids,
Splashed with grey,
Like the grey foggy mist on a winter's morning,
Like the feathers on a seagull.
That is the colour of my eyes.

Barrie Creamer (9)
St Leonard's Primary School, East Kilbride

HAPPINESS

Happiness is getting a new Godzilla toy.
Happiness is ice-cream on a hot day.
Happiness is going to the country on my bike.
Happiness is visiting my cousins.
Happiness is going on holidays.
Happiness is going to see Doctor Dolittle in the cinema.

Daniel Cummiskey (8)
St Leonard's Primary School, East Kilbride

EYES

My eyes are a cold dark brown
As brown as chocolate melting in the pot
Or coffee with nothing in it
Speckled with red and yellow
As red as a sunset on a summer's day
As yellow as buttercups dancing in the wind
That is the colours of my eyes.

Jaimie Miller (9)
St Leonard's Primary School, East Kilbride

MY FAVOURITE ANIMAL

Touching a pair of velvet ears,
Stroking her soft silk fur,
Alsatians are her only fear,
To me, she's a dream come true!

When dinner is ready she licks her lips,
Drooling and begging for some,
For pizza, rice and chicken dips,
To me, she's a dream come true!

Running around and bouncing her ball,
Up and down the park,
She's a bundle of laughter and fun for all,
To me, she's a dream come true!

Swimming in water is what she loves,
She could splash about all day,
Playing around with my big bruv,
To me, she's a dream come true!

She's always excited to come to my house,
She runs and jumps like mad,
But when she gets tired she's as quiet as a mouse,
But she's still like a dream come true!

She's been my best friend for six whole years,
She's the best dog who's ever lived,
If she wasn't around I would be in tears,
She is of course my dog *Holly!*

Laura Brannan (11)
St Leonard's Primary School, East Kilbride

THE CHASE

The gleaming, glittering eyes,
Set above his black-tipped nose
Searching for prey.
There he stood,
Silhouetted against the dawn light
On the brink of the hill.
The fox!

Far-off in the distance,
A hunting horn sounds, signalling danger.
The sharp ears prick up,
Suddenly alert.
He senses the vibrations of the horses' hooves
Thundering along the ground.

Far from his den,
He darts through the trees,
Frantically searching for cover.
He hears the panting of the hounds.
Hot on his trail,
And the voices of their masters,
Calling to them, ordering them
To hunt him down.

The hot breath of the hounds
Is now on his back,
And they are snapping at his heels.
He sees his den just through the trees
With new-found energy, he races towards it.
He's got to make it!
He reaches it, exhausted, the hunter's outrun.

Alexandra Carney (12)
St Leonard's Primary School, East Kilbride

THE MOON

I wonder how the moon's so high
away way up in the sky.
How so bright up in space?
I think I saw a little face.

Watching rockets zooming by,
I wonder how they really fly,
Launching satellites they will do
I wonder if they catch the flu?

Only the rope to keep them still,
I wonder if the aliens get ill?
Astronauts walking on the moon,
I hope they will be home soon.

Adam McDonald (9)
St Marnock's Primary School, Glasgow

PUDDING PIE

Pudding pie, pudding pie
Would you like to try?

It's nice and it's yummy
Pudding pie, pudding pie.

Care for a bite?
You wouldn't like to fight
Pudding pie, pudding pie.

The pudding's done
And that was fun
Pudding pie, pudding pie.

Laura Smith (9)
St Marnock's Primary School, Glasgow

MY BED

My bed is very comfortable,
My bed is very hot.
But after all my bed,
Is the best of the lot.
I sit on the spot,
Where it is very, very hot.

And after a while it gets really, really hot.
In the morning when I wake,
I never ever want to get up.
When I go to school I do my work,
And then I get my tuck.

Robyn Kilcullen (8)
St Marnock's Primary School, Glasgow

PANDAS

Pandas, pandas, black and white,
Have good teeth but never bite,
You will never see them fight,
Unless you give them a nasty fright.

Pandas, pandas, climb up trees,
Under fur have knobbly knees,
But they never like the bees,
So they go back down the trees.

Pandas, pandas are down to please,
Don't put them in a zoo,
They were here before you,
So leave them some bamboo to chew.

Nichola Morris (9)
St Marnock's Primary School, Glasgow

SNOW

The snow falls to the ground
Streets and houses too.
It melts on my ears and nose and toes
Then I go home with a nasty nasty flu.

Then next day I can't go to school
And in my bed it is not fun like school.
Oh I hope I get better, oh I hope I will
Get better soon and go back to school.

Playing in the snow is not really fun
because you probably like the hot hot sun
Last year in January it was snowing
I came in and Grandad said come and do the mowing.

Stephanie Grattan (8)
St Marnock's Primary School, Glasgow

BIRDS

Birds, birds don't eat bees,
But they live in trees,
They build nests with twigs,
And leaves.

Birds fly through the sky,
But some birds don't eat pies,
But they do like the nice blue skies.

Robert McCreath (9)
St Marnock's Primary School, Glasgow

BIRDS

Birds are small and birds are big
And they can die in an oil rig
They dig for juicy worms
But worms make me squirm

Birds hate bumblebees
But they take them at their ease
And they love the green leaves
That shine in the big green trees

Birds are black and white
But there they are not scared of heights
And they always sing at night
When it isn't really bright

Birds can fly so high
That they nearly touch the sky
And they never say goodbye
And they never tell a lie

Birds stay up till dawn
And they fly about all morn
And they're little when they're born
And they hate the great big storm.

Jamie McCann (9)
St Marnock's Primary School, Glasgow

THE MOON

The moon shines
Like candlelight
And when I look I always say
'The sun's been here today'
And go back inside to play.

The moon shines with sky light
And when I come home from dancing
I see the moon sometimes half sometimes full
And sometimes I don't see one at all.

Samantha Ward (8)
St Marnock's Primary School, Glasgow

THE RIVER NILE

The River Nile,
Makes Egyptians smile,
Because it waters crops.
The River Nile,
Will be there for quite a while,
Because it runs through Egypt from bottom to top.

The Nile is free,
To Egypt and me,
We all like that river.
But if you drive,
Right into a dive,
It will make you shiver.

If it wasn't for the Nile,
No Egyptians would smile,
And there would be no Egyptian land.
It would be bad,
And very sad,
If the Nile was banned.

Rachael McCreadie (9)
St Marnock's Primary School, Glasgow

DREAMS

Sometimes as I lay in bed
I see birds flying round my head
When I wake up I know it's a dream
But if it's scary I'm sure to scream.

A dream is made up in your head
But comes true in your bed
In my dreams I have a cat
A hamster, dog and a rat.

If one of my dreams is extra good
I wake up in a lovely mood
I shout and scream with all my might
And then I can't wait till night! night! night!

I hate to have a scary dream
Because all the monsters make me scream
But lovely dreams I just don't know
Why they have to go go go.

In my dream one time
I saw a walking lime
Sometimes I am rich
And all my money I will spend
Until my dream comes to an end.

Kayleigh McMahon (9)
St Marnock's Primary School, Glasgow

BUILDINGS

Schools are small schools are tall.
Schools are any kind of building at all.
Teachers teach you how to read and write
And lots lots more to think about.

Houses are small houses are tall.
Houses are any kind of buildings at all.
Houses are cosy, houses are comfortable.
Houses are fun for exploring about.

Flats are small flats are tall.
Flats are any kind of buildings at all.
Some flats have three verandas
And some have lots lots more.

Hotels are small hotels are tall.
Hotels are any kind of buildings at all.
Hotels are lovely hotels are cosy.
Hotels are tidy to have a drink in.

Theatres are small theatres are tall.
Theatres are any kind of buildings at all.
You go to theatres to watch and listen
And not for a christening.

Churches are small churches are tall.
Churches are any kind of buildings at all.
You go to church to watch and listen
And I like it when it is a christening.

Claire McManus (8)
St Marnock's Primary School, Glasgow

ANIMALS

They come in all different shapes and sizes.
Red, blue and green galore,
Then off to bed just as the sun rises,
So go to the zoo if you want to see some more.

You'll find wild animals in the jungle, pets at home,
Goldfish in tanks,
And little creatures like lizards
Stand there still as a gnome.

My favourites are the big cats,
Because of their golden skin
But don't forget the blood-sucking bats
Because they have wings.

And don't forget the snakes,
Because they swim in the lakes,
And the puppy dogs
Because they croak like frogs.

Stephanie Gow (8)
St Marnock's Primary School, Glasgow

IF YOU SHOULD MEET A TIGER

If you should meet a tiger
That is orange with black stripes
Don't run away from it
Don't be scared of it
Or he will eat you for dinner.

Wesun Kraish (9)
St Patrick's Primary School, Glasgow

IF YOU SHOULD MEET A SHARK

If you should meet a shark,
Yes, oh yes a shark,
Please keep calm,
Break a tile, then run a mile,
Then when you've ran that mile,
Don't give a smile,
Because he'll come after a while,
His big jaggy fin,
Will make you shiver like a jelly,
Yes, oh yes that's a shark.

Sharon Bruce (10)
St Patrick's Primary School, Glasgow

IF YOU MEET A DRAGON

If you meet a dragon
You should run like the wind.
Or if you are brave you
should stand up to him
But that is not a good idea
Because he will set you on fire
And he will say 'This is meat
And it is time to eat.'

Charles Cullen (10)
St Patrick's Primary School, Glasgow

IF YOU MEET A HORSE

If you meet a horse
Who runs like the wind
Who jumps and runs
And rolls over the grass
And pushes you off his back
His colour of body is pure black
He has big strong bones
So he can't break his back
So if you meet a horse
The same as him
He will be your pal.

Marc McCann (10)
St Patrick's Primary School, Glasgow

IF YOU SHOULD MEET A BEAR

If you should meet a bear,
Don't run away in a scare,
Just play dead so he won't know,
That he's just let dinner go.
He's big, he's fierce, he's brown and he's strong,
So if you don't play dead, he will just eat you up!

Steven Monaghan (10)
St Patrick's Primary School, Glasgow

IF YOU SHOULD MEET A BUMBLEBEE

If you should meet a bumblebee,
Don't disturb its home tree.
For it does no harm making honey,
Especially when it's in your tummy.
So a word of warning,
If you should see a bee buzzing,
Don't harm it or you will have
No honey in your tummy.

Rosaleen Bans (10)
St Patrick's Primary School, Glasgow

IF YOU SHOULD MEET AN ANT

If you should meet an ant,
Don't go over and stand on it,
Watch the way it crawls around
On its four legs and four feet
When it tries to hurry
Its head wiggles from side to side,
So if you meet an ant
Don't crush it with your foot.

Ashley McIntosh (10)
St Patrick's Primary School, Glasgow

My Cousin

My cousin is cool
He likes to play the fool
Out all day he's allowed to stay
He's tough
He's rough
He always pinches my stuff!

Mark McCarron (10)
St Timothy's Primary School, Glasgow

My Dream

When I was young and very small
I could walk and run and play football.
Ever since, my only dream
Is to play for my favourite football team.

Mark Burke (10)
St Timothy's Primary School, Glasgow

Ted

I have a bear called Ted
He sits at the end of my bed.
When he sleeps at night I hear him snore
But it's better than hearing him roar.

Nicola Morley (10)
St Timothy's Primary School, Glasgow

HORSES

Some horses are tough,
Some horses are rough,
Some horses are mad,
Some horses are bad,
Some horses are sweet,
Most horses like to eat,
Lots of minty sweets
And lots of other treats.

Sarah Quinn (10)
St Timothy's Primary School, Glasgow

SISTERS

S isters are fine for a while
I n some cases they make you smile
S ome are young some are old
T hey don't always do as they are told
E ven when you argue and fight
R emember she loves you with all her might
Sisters.

Natalie Mackin (10)
St Timothy's Primary School, Glasgow

HOW WOULD YOU FEEL?

How would you feel if
You couldn't tell someone you were hurt?
You were kept in a cage?
You did the same thing every day?
You ate the same thing every day?
How would you feel?

Emma Brown (11)
Scotstoun Primary School, Glasgow

A DOG'S LIFE

How would you feel if you had to
sleep on a cold kitchen floor?
You had to wear a collar?
You were hit on the nose?
You had to sleep in a cold kennel?
How would you feel?

Michael Rogers (10)
Scotstoun Primary School, Glasgow

LIKE A HAMSTER

How would you feel if . . .
You got put in a plastic ball and made to run around?
You lived in a cage full of sawdust?
You got picked up all the time and patted and played with?
You got taken away from your family and bought?
How would you feel?

Chloe Beck (10)
Scotstoun Primary School, Glasgow

BEING A TERRAPIN

How would you feel if
You had to swim in the water you did the toilet in?
You ate food that landed in the dirty water?
You had to put up with the smell of your tank every day?
You got picked up when you didn't want to be?
How would *you* feel?

Matthew Sharkey (10)
Scotstoun Primary School, Glasgow

HOW WOULD YOU!

How would you feel if
You could not tell someone you were hurt?
You had to sleep *outside?*
You had to stay in a cage?
You got disturbed when you were sleeping?
How would you feel?

Lauren Turner (10)
Scotstoun Primary School, Glasgow

HOW WOULD YOU FEEL IF YOU WERE A DOG

How would you feel if
You had to wear a muzzle?
You had to eat in a dark corner of the kitchen?
You couldn't tell someone you were hurt?
You had to sleep in a kennel?
How would you feel?

Craig Worton (10)
Scotstoun Primary School, Glasgow

BEING TORTURED

How would you feel if,
You had to wear an old lead every time
you go outside?
You had to be dragged around streets
every day of your life?
You had no voice and couldn't say
'For goodness sake leave me alone!'
You had to put up with a life of
Being fed disgusting food every day!
How would *you* feel?

Sarah Rhodes (10)
Scotstoun Primary School, Glasgow

A LIFE OF A RABBIT

How would you feel if
You had to get picked up by the ears?
You had to live in a hutch?
You had to eat so many vegetables?
You were not allowed to run about or go out to play?
How would you feel?

Paul McGinlay (10)
Scotstoun Primary School, Glasgow

IT'S A DOG'S LIFE

How would you feel if
You had to sleep on a cold floor?
You had to eat off the floor?
You had to stay in a kennel every night?
You had to wear a muzzle?
How would you feel?

Stuart Barclay (10)
Scotstoun Primary School, Glasgow

MY DOG

My dog is very lazy
My dog acts very young
She even walks around
As if she's only even one.

She hates going to the vet
And watching small cats too.
People say she's very sweet
And others just say *shoo!*

She makes a mess around the house
And barks all the time
She annoys every other dog
But sometimes she's just fine!

Mhairi Morrison (11)
Shawlands Primary School

THE STARS AT NIGHT

The stars at night are very bright
Like glitter in the sky,
They shine, they twinkle and they gleam
As if it were a dream,
But sometimes I sit by the window
And wonder how bright they could be,
And sometimes stars can be so small
That I can hardly see,
But the main question of all is
Why do they twinkle?
If anyone knows can you please tell me?

Saima Butt (11)
Shawlands Primary School

MY SPECIAL FAMILY AND FRIENDS

My family are very special to me,
My mum, my dad, my sisters.
My close friends are also special to me,
But not as special as my family.
My sisters they fight but not for long
Because they are special to each other.
Me and my friends sometimes argue
But not for long when we find what's wrong.

Clair Nicholson (12)
Shawlands Primary School

UNDER THE BED

Under the bed I never go.
There's a scary monster down there.
At night when I am lying in bed,
I hear deep breathing.
It's the monster.
There is a dark shadow under there.
I know if I look something bad will happen.
I hide under my covers until I get to sleep.
I am scared of the monster.
Morning, please come.

Eleanor Poyner (11)
Shawlands Primary School

FRIENDSHIP

Friendship is a wonderful thing to have
With a best friend you could share things with each other
and you could keep each other's secrets
You can see your friends at school every day and at weekends
If you communicate with other people you can find yourself friends
Friends could do things for you like doing you a big favour
They could also be there for you when you are down
Or when you are hurt by someone
Or somebody you are not close to.

Sadia Shakoor (11)
Shawlands Primary School

ZOMBIES

Are they dead or are they alive?
Who would know except their wives.
Who would want their worthless lives,
If they are dead, but are they alive?

They will try to steal your blood,
They will trample on some mud,
They act like tiny lizards,
But will they be caught in a blizzard?

First you see a little bee,
Then you have a cup of tea,
What do you think you will see
When you see a pack of zombies?

Jonathan Li (11)
Shawlands Primary School

I LIKE TO PLAY IN THE PARK

I like to play in the park because it is just so good.
I like the swings because they just go so high.
I also like the slide when it goes fast.
But when it goes slow I don't like it.
The best bit is when the ice-cream van comes
Because I can buy sweets and orange ice lollies,
Because they are yummy for my tummy.

Neelim Gill (11)
Shawlands Primary School

GHOSTS

Ghosts are creatures that stalk the Earth
Looking for houses to haunt.
They appear at night to give you a fright.
Some are good, some are bad.
A few are just lonely and sad.
They just want someone to talk to.
Some go to heaven, some go to hell.
Others slam doors and ring your bells.
If you see one don't be scared,
They're mostly just as harmless as a baby bear.

Ryan McCaig (11)
Shawlands Primary School

MY GRANDAD

My grandad was always jolly
and always gave me a lolly
My grandad was always very kind
he didn't do much but I didn't mind
My grandad's name was Willie
and he was always silly
My grandad died in 1997
and now he's up there in heaven.

Iain Hamilton (11)
Shawlands Primary School

When I Was Little

When I was little
I was so sweet and soft
I dreamt of being a football player
And still dream of that today.

When I was little
I walked before I crawled
Although I fell quite often
I'm very proud of it.

When I was little
I never cried and screamed
I was so very quiet
And never bawled out loud.

When I was little
I called my bottle 'Tup'
It was always full of milk
And I always gobbled it up.

Now that I'm grown up
I look back and think
I did such good things
When I was little.

Neil Dinnen (11)
Shawlands Primary School

War

W orrying
he A rtbreaking
 w R ong.

Myles Gilpin (11)
Shawlands Primary School

EVACUATION

It's cold and dirty
Dark and smelly too
The people that I live with don't have a clue
That I'm asthmatic and can't work the farm
Yesterday I nearly didn't have an arm
Rake here, rake there. Do this, do that, I'm sick of it
I can smell a rat
They're never in they're always out
The only thing they call me is riech un gourt
It was only today that I realised
It can't be, it has to be
They're German spies!
I can't do anything, I have to do something
I'll write to my mother
She'll know what to do
If only she had a clue
I shouldn't have gone
I should have stayed home!

Anthony Dowridge (11)
Shawlands Primary School

UNITED FOREVER

My favourite club is Man United
for they are the best.
Yorkie is their best player
he even scored two against Inter.
This year I think they'll win it all
and that's why I'll support United forever.

Andrew Sheddon (11)
Shawlands Primary School

GRAN

She is nice and kind.
I hardly ever see her.
She stay quite far away
But when I do see her, it is really really fun.
She is a really good gran.
She has to be the best out of all in the world.
She is so special.
She is great.
She has four dogs.
They are all boys but one.
She is a girl called Faith.
They are all special to my gran
Like everyone in our family.
She loves us all the same.

Lisa Garrity (11)
Shawlands Primary School

MY GRANDAD

My grandad likes to get up from his bed
to make his breakfast at nine
and he would love a glass of wine.
At ten he sits and has a little smoke
on his big brown pipe.
Then goes out for a drink in the mission at 10.30am.
After he's had a drink he starts to go and get brunch.
A bowl of hot tomato soup, then a plate of steak.
For then his desert a bowl of chocolate cake and custard.
Finally he takes a walk home and takes a flip with a kip
Zzzzzzzz.

Leah McKee (11)
Shawlands Primary School

CHILD OF THE PAST, CHILD OF THE PRESENT

Child of the past
Sad and lonely

Child of the present
With happiness only

Child of the past
With lots of jobs to do

Child of the present
Watching Doctor Who

Child of the past
Eating a lot of gruel

Child of the present
Eating something nice and cool

Child of the past
Living in hell

Child of the present
Waiting for the school bell.

David Wilson (9)
Shawlands Primary School

STRAWBERRIES

A strawberry is plump, speckled and round
They grow from a plant in the ground.
Having strawberries with cream
Is something like a dream.
I think strawberries are a treat
Because they are good to eat.

Lynsey-Anne Hutchison (11)
Shawlands Primary School

VICTORIAN

V ictoria was the Queen
I n fancy dresses
C limbing into a carriage
T all as can be
O pposite of ugly
R ight all the time
I 'll, hardly ever
A lways very polite
N ever rude at any time.

Claire Brown (10)
Shawlands Primary School

SKIING

Up in the morning
tired and yawning
getting ready to ski.

Then out into cold air,
mountains, rocks and snow.
We see blue skies ahead.

Slipping, sliding and gliding,
everyone is falling.
It's great fun so come!

Linda Duncan (10)
Shawlands Primary School

THE ROBOT CHICKENS

All our chickens are useless
There's nothing in their heads
All they do is lie around
And wait to go to bed

Then Dad made Robo-cluck
A marvellous machine
He's very very brainy
And gets your clothes clean

He lays eggs all day
He walks where he pleases
All his eggs are extremely fresh
They make wonderful cheeses

Robo-cluck is wonderful
He's the best on my farm
He's so very clever he can even . . .
knit from balls of yarn.

David McMahon (10)
Shawlands Primary School

THE MAD MAN

The mad man called Mike
Had a bike
Pink and white
He likes riding on the bike
He bumps into people and falls.
Everyone panics when he is about
on his bike.

Anisa Mushtaq (10)
Shawlands Primary School

ANIMALS

Animals animals everywhere
Animals animals in the air
Some are big some are small
Some are short and some are tall

Animals animals on the land
Animals animals in the sand
Some are brown some are grey
Some like to live in hay

Animals animals in the sea
Animals animals eating tea
Some are wild some are pets
Some hate going to the vets.

Anna MacNaughton (10)
Shawlands Primary School

THE FLY

This little fly that buzzes by
Spreads diseases wherever it pleases.

After the fly the man did caper
And tried to swat it with a newspaper.

At last the man had hit the fly
It fell to the floor and started to die.

The little fly that buzzed by
Lies on the floor spreading diseases no more.

Keith McDonald (10)
Shawlands Primary School

At The Fair

I love going to the fair
You get ice-cream and candy that sticks to your hair
I like winning coconuts and giving them to Dad
When I win teddies, I give them to my sister
As soon as she sees them she just calls them 'Mister'
I like going on big rides
My favourite is the Ocean Tides
My mum feels sick when she's on them
But I think they're easy
I hate it when we go home
The fun just stops like that
But I know I'll be back.

Scott Jeffrey (10)
Shawlands Primary School

Swimming

Every Friday after school
I go swimming in the pool
I dive into the pool with such a splash
That everyone runs and cuts a dash
I swim and jump and dive galore
I don't want it to end, I want more and more
But at eight o'clock we have to get out
I don't want to but I don't scream and shout
I have a shower and then get dressed
And think that today has been the best!

Paul Leinster (10)
Shawlands Primary School

ANIMALS

Animals they are full of fun
Most of them love to run.
Smooth ones, fluffy ones
Scratchy ones too,
We should love them and care for them
Me and you.
The lion with its furry mane,
The ostrich that runs faster than a train.
The hamster who scampers around,
The mole that burrows underground.
They're all so different, how lucky we are,
There are animals everywhere, near and far.
Elephants, lions, monkeys too,
You can go and see them all in the zoo.

Nadine Calder (10)
Shawlands Primary School

BLESS THIS MESS

My mum and dad are sad,
My sisters have blisters,
My dog licks the bog,
I am nice,
The cat has lice,
How old are you?
The dog's turned blue.

Alex Finlay (10)
Shawlands Primary School

ON HOLIDAY

Going on holiday is always fun,
A brilliant treat for everyone.
This time we're going to the Bahamas,
Pineapples, coconuts and bananas.

The sea was clear,
The sand was golden,
Our hotel was not an old one,
Then we decided to go exploring.

There were lots of animals to be found,
The best I think
Was a curling snake,
That made my mother shiver and shake!

But all good things
Must come to an end,
We're flying home
To our friends.

Joanne Cairns (10)
Shawlands Primary School

VICTORIAN WORKHOUSE

I see a big unwelcoming building with big gates in front of it.
I hear children crying because they want their parents.
I feel upset because I can't see my family.
I touch the little bit of food I get with my spoon.
I wish I didn't live here because I never get to see my family.

Adele Suzanne Neilson (10)
Shawlands Primary School

SPIDERS

Spider spider don't come near
My big sister has a fear.
You climb up walls and live in webs
Normal spiders have got eight legs.

Spider spider don't come near
My big sister has a fear.
You sit for hours on the walls
And she screams if you fall.

Spider spider don't come near
My big sister has a fear.
Ignore her and crawl away
Don't come back another day.

Alan Bain (10)
Shawlands Primary School

DOLPHINS

D olphins are fun
O ut in the sea
L aughing and talking
P orpoising and playing
H appy and joyful
I n the water
N o one hates them
        We all love them
                And they love us.

Kirin Malhi (10)
Shawlands Primary School

AT THE FAIR

At the fair, at the fair
Having fun, having fun
While we go on rides that are really fun
My dad eats a sticky bun
Throwing balls at coconuts
Winning prizes, winning prizes
On the rollercoaster
On the dodgems too
Inside the Haunted House
I hear my mum scream
I'm really high on the Big Wheel
But I'm scared of heights
I've really had a day of fun
But now the day is done.

Jamie McKenna (10)
Shawlands Primary School

CHILDREN

C hildren are fun
H appy all day
I   am one
L ying in the sun
D ancing at parties
R unning when playing games
E ating food greedily
N ow time for bed.

Alan McLaren (10)
Shawlands Primary School

MY HORSE CLOVER

I have a horse called Clover.
He eats a lot of grass and drinks a lot of water.
In summer he lives at the River Endrick
and watches the salmon jumping
out of and back into the water.

In winter he lives in Dumgoyne,
letting out lots of dung,
which helps the farmers
on the land,
to grow crops
which are vital
for our tummies.

My horse Clover will not bite,
but will give you the slightest nibble,
but do not go -
I was just joking.
He wouldn't really hurt a fly
for he is just a great big softie,
lumbering round and round.

I love Clover with all my heart,
and I hope he loves me with his.

Katie O'Brien (11)
Shawlands Primary School

VICTORIAN FACTORY

I see young people working at machinery.
I hear lots of loud and noisy sounds.
I feel tired and sore.
I touch the cold metal with my hands.
I wish I was somewhere else.

Jamie Morrison (10)
Shawlands Primary School

TAY RAIL BRIDGE DISASTER

I see debris from the train and bridge, even bodies.
I hear the screams from people and the whistling of the wind.
I touch the debris and bodies in the water.
I feel the cold wind and water on my face.
I wish this disaster never happened.
I hope that there are some survivors in this wreck.

Jack O'Brien (11)
Shawlands Primary School

VICTORIAN WORKHOUSE

I see lots of other children.
I hear a lot of the kids crying for their mums.
I feel the thin blankets covering me.
I touch the food with my spoon.
I wish I was cuddling my mum.

Amy Wallace (10)
Shawlands Primary School

TAY BRIDGE DISASTER

I see the wreckage of the bridge in the water.
I hear the clashing of water.
I touch the rocks I am sitting on.
I feel very sad for the people that died.
I wish that there were survivors.
I hope that it doesn't happen again.

Laurie Brown (10)
Shawlands Primary School

HANNAH IN A VICTORIAN MANSION

I see lots of rooms, beautiful dolls and lovely dresses.
I hear the tinkling of cutlery, Mrs Arkwright giving orders
and the horse-driven carriages.
I touch the fine clothes, the dolls and the lovely soft beds.
I feel safe and happy but a little homesick.
I wish I was rich and lived in a house like this.

John Peter Winchester (10)
Shawlands Primary School

TAY BRIDGE DISASTER

I see the bridge and train as it falls into the murky river.
The iron snaps like a twig.
I hear the people screaming and the clatter of the storm.
I feel very shocked because it is all very sudden.
I wish the train and bridge did not fall and the people would live.
I hope the rescuers would recover the people in the train.

Sam Duncan (10)
Shawlands Primary School

WINTERTIME IS . . .

The sight of white soft snow falling from the sky.
The sight of children cuddling in beside the fire.

The sound of laughter as children play in the snow.
The sound of feet crunching in the snow.

The taste of snowballs in your mouth.
The taste of hot cocoa.

The feel of the freezing cold.
The feel of numb fingers and toes.

The smell of beautiful fresh air.
The smell of smoke from a car.

Lynsey Latimer (9)
Stepps Primary School

IF . . .

If my dad was a tree
He would be an oak
Standing big and strong

If my dad was a pot of paint
He would be black
To make everyone angry

If my dad was an animal
He would be a woodpecker
Making noise, banging where he went.

Diane McKay (9)
Stepps Primary School

IF . . .

If my mum was an animal
She'd be a puppy
Caring, with a brown shiny coat
Always licking my face.

If my mum was a drink
She'd be water
Ice-cold and lovely to drink
Always trying to keep fresh.

If my mum was a pot of paint
She'd be a blue pot
Joyful and stroking happiness
Leading the way to the sky.

Lisa Markey (9)
Stepps Primary School

IF . . .

If my mum was a bird
She would be a dove
Bright and wise and swooping
In and out the tall trees.

If my mum was a fruit
She would be an orange
Bright and joyful
Rolling around in the sun.

If my mum were a flower
She would be a rose
Tall and straight
And as bright as the sun.

David Thomson (9)
Stepps Primary School

BULLIES

It's just not fair,
They always pick on me,
It's just not fair,
Will they ever let me be?
It is so terrible,
It really is unbearable,
But when it turns 3 o'clock,
I have something to fear.
They're always waiting at the gate,
Kicking and shouting right in my ear,
When I get home and have blood on my face,
And my mum says 'What's wrong dear?'
My heart starts to race.
So I told my Headmaster,
Who did his normal good,
And called them to his office,
But they were very rude.
They said I was lying,
I was a lying, horrid cheat,
They said that I was telling fibs
And I was talking through my feet.
So I ran and ran and ran and ran,
Because I didn't know what to do,
But that's when suddenly I came across you.
It feels a lot better though, when I talk to someone,
I'm going to stand up to those bullies,
Though I won't become one.

Jessica Louise O'Neill Murray (9)
Stepps Primary School

IF . . .

If my mum were a flower
She'd be a red red rose
Swaying side to side
Glistening like glass in the sun.

If my mum were a pot of paint
She'd be a sparkling peach colour
Always smiling, happy and bright
Opening the doorway to life.

If my mum were an animal
She'd be a dolphin
Dipping in and out
Of the bluest sea.

If my mum were a drink
She'd be a tropical punch
Trickling down your throat, soothing it
On a hot summer's day.

Emma Hazelton (9)
Stepps Primary School

IF

If my mum was a flower
She'd be a daffodil
Bright and beautiful
Dancing in the spring breeze.

If my mum was a pet
She'd be a guinea pig
Scurrying quickly place to place
But hiding away from strangers.

If my mum was a pot of paint
She'd be bright yellow
Putting a cheerful smile to
Everyone's face.

If my mum was an animal
She'd be a dolphin
Swooping in and out of the clear sea
With a grin on her face.

Kevin McMinn (9)
Stepps Primary School

IF . . .

If my aunt was an animal
She would be a cat
Soft and friendly, funny
But clever and smart.

If my aunt was a pot of paint
She would be yellow
Bright and happy
Painting the world beautifully.

If my aunt was a flower
She would be a snowdrop
Small and pretty
Quietly dancing in the wind.

If my aunt was a tree
She would be an oak
Strong and sturdy
Caring for birds on her branches.

Megan Duff (10)
Stepps Primary School

SUMMERTIME IS . . .

The sight of the bees
Humming away to a beautiful tune,

The sight of the beach
Sunny and fair making me smile,

The sound of dogs
Barking in the hot sun,

The sound of splashing water
Cooling and refreshing warm faces,

The taste of tangy juice
Refreshing and very satisfying,

The taste of cool ice-cream
Welcoming experience down the side of your throat,

The smell of hot-dogs
Sizzling and sparkling making my mouth water,

The smell of the flowers
Sweet and tall,

The feel of the fresh cut grass
Soft, warm and bouncy,

The feel of the smooth sand
Running through my fingers

Summertime is everything!

Natalie C Long (9)
Stepps Primary School

Wintertime Is . . .

The sight of icicles dripping off my window,
The sight of the snowman waiting for someone to come.

The sound of children laughing happily outside,
The sound of my mum telling me to put my hat on yet again.

The taste of hot soup trickling down my throat,
The taste of hot chestnuts burning my mouth.

The smell of my dinner wafting from the kitchen,
The smell of fresh air out in the garden.

The feel of the snow seeping through my gloves,
The feel of my cold body shivering in the cold.

Marisa Kerr (9)
Stepps Primary School

If . . .

If my mum was a flower,
She would be a red red rose,
Strong but lovely,
Dancing in the wind.

If my mum was a pot of paint,
She would be yellow,
Painting some life into everyone.

If my mum was a drink,
She would be water,
Kind to all,
Running in her path.

Emma-Louise Hutchison (9)
Stepps Primary School

IF . . .

If my mum was an animal
She'd be a sparrow
Petite with brown shiny feathers
Always flitting through the trees.

If my mum was a tree
She'd be a willow
Big narrow standing proudly
When the wind comes she would
Swing with the air.

If my mum was a flower
She'd be a tulip
Making everybody happy and joyful
When the wind comes she
Sways with it peacefully.

Catherine O'Brien (9)
Stepps Primary School

IF . . .

If my brother was an animal
He'd be a gerbil
Fast and funny with brown fur
Always being suspicious

If my brother was a pot of paint
He'd be scarlet red
Bursting with rage
And ruling the house

If my brother was a drink
He'd be some lemonade
Crackly and fizzy
And very tangy

If my brother was a tree
He'd be a holly tree
Sharp and jaggy
But reliable.

Andy Paterson (9)
Stepps Primary School

IF

If my grandpa was an animal
He'd be a swan
A very angry one
Standing proud and strong.

If my grandpa was a fruit
He'd be a melon
Very sour and very nippy
In the fruit bowl.

If my grandpa was a tree
He'd be a big oak
Mostly very strong
Standing fat and tall.

David Hunter (9)
Stepps Primary School

If . . .

If my mum was a fruit
She'd be a watermelon
All juicy and sweet
And refreshing in your mouth.

But

If my mum was a flower
She'd be a daffodil
Dancing away in the mid summer breeze
And always kind and thoughtful.

Or maybe

If my mum was a drink
She'd be a glass of lemonade
Giving you a cool tangy taste
And always fizzing up.

Eilidh Gordon (9)
Stepps Primary School

School Is . . .

The sight of children playing tig,
The sight of games painted on the playground.

The sound of children munching and crunching crisps,
The sound of girls playing recorders loud and long.

The taste of blackcurrant jelly with ice-cream
Wibbling and wobbling down into my belly.
The taste of orange juice running down my throat
In a hot summer's day.

The smell of the toilets, rotten and remember to use tissue paper.
The smell of cheese and onion crisps floating
Around the fresh air in the classroom.

The feel of chalk slipping through my smooth fingers.
The feel of a chair smooth and maybe rare.

Robert Cruickshank (9)
Stepps Primary School

WINTERTIME IS . . .

The sight of the snow covering the grass
The sight of the icicles flaking and dripping off
The windows like a freezing cold tap.

The sound of the children playing in the snow
Making it crunch ever so.
The sound of the man scraping the freezing cold ice
Off his little blue car.

The taste of the hot chocolate hot and sweet
Making you have a good nights sleep.
The taste of the fresh air making our face cold
Even though it's freezing cold.

The smell of the wood burning away in the
Midnight fire just a few minutes away.
The smell of the ice making my tummy rumble
In the sparkling cold night.

The feel of the fire on my skin making me
Warm and tingly.
The feel of the brightness trying to make
Tomorrow another fresh day.

Courtney Donaldson (10)
Stepps Primary School

SWIMMING BATHS IS . . .

The sight of the pool, not relaxing having fun,
The sight of the slides, people rushing past in the sun.

The sound of the children yelling screaming loud and long,
The sound of waves crashing up and down as if
Dancing to a song.

The taste of the water horrible and strong,
The taste of your drink in your throat so long.

The smell of the chlorine on your wet nose,
The smell of the food teasing my tummy.

The feel of the wrinkles like an old lady,
The feel of the cold floor straight out of the pool.

Lorna Nicolson (9)
Stepps Primary School

IF . . .

If my mum was an animal
She'd be a cat
Waiting patiently for food
With kind glowing eyes and shiny fur

If my mum was a pot of paint
She'd be laughing lemon
Loyal and funny
Stroking happiness to everyone

If my mum was a flower
She'd be a rose
Because she has rosy cheeks
And always helpful to bees buzzing by.

Lauren Smith (9)
Stepps Primary School

IN SPACE

The spinning rings
The floating asteroids
The golden sun
The rocky moon
The bright stars
The big spaceship
The flashing lights
The slimy aliens
The round planets
The floating spaceman
The fresh air
The big planet
The black galaxy
The red planet
The Milky Way
The small planet Pluto.

Donna McOnie (11)
Sunnyside Primary School

BLACK AND WHITE

We should all play together
And be good friends.
We stay with pals some nights
And we never ever have fights.
We all grow at our own pace
And we are all in the human race.
We might have a different face
But we have the same heart
So we don't all drift apart.
If we cut our hand we have the same blood
If we all fall we'd get covered.in mud.
Older kids go to clubs
Or adults can even go to pubs.
They may have different cultures
And they may have different language
But underneath we're all the same
Even if we have different names.
We may have names like James or Jim
They may have names like Tom or Tim.
Well bye from me, maybe next time we'll see
Black's the same as white and I hope we won't fight.

Christine Douglas (11)
Sunnyside Primary School

BLACK AND WHITE

We might be black
We might be white
We might be dark
We might be bright.
Why we fight I do not know
So let us play like Tinky Winky
Dipsy, Laa-Laa and Po.

We like Indian food
So let's give some respect.
Please don't fight
So get it right

We are all the same!

Tony Paterson (11)
Sunnyside Primary School

MY EYES

My eyes are as green as the grass
on a summer's night
with flickers of white like a fish
gliding through the water with the sun
hitting its shiny body
my eyes have a spark of orange
like a fire in the middle of my eyes
with flickers of yellow like the sun bouncing off.

Chevonne McOnie (10)
Sunnyside Primary School

LET'S ALL PLAY TOGETHER

Let's all play together
Let's all get along
Don't be enemies just be friends
Share all your toys and respect others
No matter whether you're black or white
It doesn't really mater we're all the same
in different ways
We can get along if we just try
We hope that no one will every cry
There are lots of parks for us to play
The adults can come and watch all day
Don't call people names
Just be friends in different ways
Names can be hurtful
Names are sad, some people just get mad
Quit the hurt
Quit the name calling
Let's all get together and have a heart
If our parents just try to mix
Then maybe the children will do the same.

Lesley-Ann Watson (11)
Sunnyside Primary School